The Complete Guide to
Locating and Profiting from Emerging Real Estate Markets

Everything You Need to Know Explained Simply

By Maurcia DeLean Houck

THE COMPLETE GUIDE TO LOCATING AND PROFITING FROM EMERGING REAL ESTATE MARKETS: EVERYTHING YOU NEED TO KNOW EXPLAINED SIMPLY

Copyright © 2011 Atlantic Publishing Group, Inc.
1405 SW 6th Avenue • Ocala, Florida 34471 • Phone 800-814-1132 • Fax 352-622-1875
Web site: www.atlantic-pub.com • E-mail: sales@atlantic-pub.com
SAN Number: 268-1250

Library of Congress Cataloging-in-Publication Data

Houck, Maurcia DeLean.
  The complete guide to locating and profiting from emerging real estate markets : everything you need to know explained simply / by Maurcia Houck.
      p. cm.
  Includes bibliographical references and index.
  ISBN-13: 978-1-60138-388-4 (alk. paper)
  ISBN-10: 1-60138-388-6 (alk. paper)
  1. Real estate investment. 2. Real estate business. I. Title.
  HD1382.5.H668 2010
  332.63'24--dc22
                          2010010847

PROJECT MANAGER: ERIN EVERHART
EDITORIAL INTERN: AMY GRONAUER
PEER REVIEW: MARILEE GRIFFIN
FRONT & BACK COVER DESIGN: JACKIE MILLER • MILLERJACKIEJ@GMAIL.COM

Printed on Recycled Paper

We recently lost our beloved pet "Bear," who was not only our best and dearest friend but also the "Vice President of Sunshine" here at Atlantic Publishing. He did not receive a salary but worked tirelessly 24 hours a day to please his parents. Bear was a rescue dog that turned around and showered myself, my wife, Sherri, his grand-

parents Jean, Bob, and Nancy, and every person and animal he met (maybe not rabbits) with friendship and love. He made a lot of people smile every day.

We wanted you to know that a portion of the profits of this book will be donated to The Humane Society of the United States. *–Douglas & Sherri Brown*

The human-animal bond is as old as human history. We cherish our animal companions for their unconditional affection and acceptance. We feel a thrill when we glimpse wild creatures in their natural habitat or in our own backyard.

Unfortunately, the human-animal bond has at times been weakened. Humans have exploited some animal species to the point of extinction.

The Humane Society of the United States makes a difference in the lives of animals here at home and worldwide. The HSUS is dedicated to creating a world where our relationship with animals is guided by compassion. We seek a truly humane society in which animals are respected for their intrinsic value, and where the human-animal bond is strong.

Want to help animals? We have plenty of suggestions. Adopt a pet from a local shelter, join The Humane Society and be a part of our work to help companion animals and wildlife. You will be funding our educational, legislative, investigative and outreach projects in the U.S. and across the globe.

Or perhaps you'd like to make a memorial donation in honor of a pet, friend or relative? You can through our Kindred Spirits program. And if you'd like to contribute in a more structured way, our Planned Giving Office has suggestions about estate planning, annuities, and even gifts of stock that avoid capital gains taxes.

Maybe you have land that you would like to preserve as a lasting habitat for wildlife. Our Wildlife Land Trust can help you. Perhaps the land you want to share is a backyard— that's enough. Our Urban Wildlife Sanctuary Program will show you how to create a habitat for your wild neighbors.

So you see, it's easy to help animals. And The HSUS is here to help.

THE HUMANE SOCIETY OF THE UNITED STATES.

2100 L Street NW • Washington, DC 20037 • 202-452-1100
www.hsus.org

Trademark

All trademarks, trade names, or logos mentioned or used are the property of their respective owners and are used only to directly describe the products being provided. Every effort has been made to properly capitalize, punctuate, identify and attribute trademarks and trade names to their respective owners, including the use of ® and ™ wherever possible and practical. Atlantic Publishing Group, Inc. is not a partner, affiliate, or licensee with the holders of said trademarks.

Table of Contents

Foreword

For some first-time real estate investors, the process of finding that ideal property, negotiating, planning, and getting the financing, is about as pleasant as a visit to the dentist. It is all extremely time consuming and stressful, not to mention emotional.

And then there are the inevitable mistakes. When I bought my first real estate investment property, I did not have a guide or any sort of plan of attack. I asked lots of questions and was forced to use my intuition along the way. Naturally, I did not always make the right moves. A few of my mistakes had substantial financial implications that I still regret to this day.

But often, those first-time buyers mature into savvy investors. They see their real estate investment as a tangible asset, over which they have direct control (unlike the stock market). With a little sweat, they can make their investment grow by painting the home, renovating the kitchen, or adding a deck to the family room. These investors revel in the knowledge that through their own efforts, they have directly impacted their bottom line. They have learned to spot real estate trends. They know where the best schools are, which neighborhoods are rising and which ones are falling, and where developers are building homes. In other words, they have caught the real estate investing "bug."

The Complete Guide to Locating and Profiting from Emerging Real Estate Markets: Everything You Need to Know Explained Simply is for all types of real estate investors, from the first-timers to the experienced. Maurcia DeLean Houck has created an easy-to-understand guide that will answer the first-time investor's questions along the way.

Of course, more experienced investors have questions, too because, if nothing else, real estate has not exactly remained stagnant over the past few years. If you have bought property, fixed it up, and realized a gain, you might be wondering what your next real estate investment move should be. Or maybe you are wondering where to invest, which property to pick, what it is like to be a landlord, how will you finance the investment, how will you deal with tenants.

The answers to these questions, and many others, are within the pages of this book. *The Complete Guide to Locating and Profiting from Emerging Real Estate Markets* leads you through the many phases of real estate investment, from the early stages of identifying emerging markets to many years later, when you decide to sell your investment property. Filled with helpful tips, wise strategies, and illuminating case studies of people who have invested in real estate dozens of times, this is an essential resource for the both the first-time and veteran inves-

tor. It will help you avoid the pitfalls of real estate investing —
and identify the possibilities.

Brendon DeSimone is a successful entrepreneur, real estate
investor, and businessman who has leveraged his expertise to
become a leading residential real estate expert.

DeSimone is regularly featured on Home and Garden Television's (HGTV) "Curb Appeal," "National Open House,"
"Bank For Your Buck," and "My House is Worth What?" When
reporting on breaking real estate news, reporters at leading
San Francisco Bay Area television news programs, as well as
national print publications, frequently seek DeSimone's expertise and savvy market perspective.

 DeSimone has transacted more than
$100 million in sales. He owns and
manages real estate in three states,
as well as in Latin America. He
started at a Silicon Valley Internet
start-up in business development
and helped grow the company
significantly before he turned his
attention and developed business
sense to real estate. DeSimone has
a proven track record of helping cli-
ents get maximum value from the purchase or sale of a residential property. Learn more at **www.brendondesimone.com.**

Introduction

Real estate prices hit historic lows. Housing market remains flat. Real estate no longer an investment. Where are the buyers? Real estate woes continue!

If you read (and believed) these headlines, you would never want to risk a penny investing in today's real estate market. Yet, thousands of smart investors are opening their wallets to buy now. Why? Because a big payoff awaits anyone willing to sit tight for a few years.

Real estate has always been considered the safest of all investments, always making at least some profit — that is, until fall 2008 when the market crashed right before our eyes. Suddenly, homeowners saw the equity in their homes disintegrate as sales prices plummeted. The word foreclosure became commonplace in many American middle- and upper-class neighborhoods. Banks froze lending. Even those with good credit and a small down payment seemed to be locked out of mortgage acquisition.

Cash became king and if you could not pay cash, you could not buy.

Fear of losing their investment monies swept the country as the real estate bubble of the early part of the decade exploded. Selling a home — any home — became virtually impossible. House flipping, a common side-job throughout the first half of the 2000s, became nonexistent, and even regular real estate investors began to rethink their investment strategy. Many wondered (and worried) if real estate investors would pull out for good, thus killing an otherwise teetering industry.

That started in 2006 but the extent of damage was not seen until Standard and Poor's S&P/Case-Shriller Home Price Indices reported the largest drop in home prices — a 19 percent decline — in its history on December 30, 2008. Prices have started to creep back up through 2009 and into 2010, steadily rising about 10 percent, and today, the outlook for real estate and its investors is much brighter. The market may remain soft, but with many experts agreeing that housing prices in many areas have hit rock bottom, investors are once again on the lookout for their next big profit-maker. Emerging markets were once limited to big cities, waterfront areas, and up-and-coming neighborhoods, but that is no longer the case. With real estate prices so low right now, almost any area could be considered an emerging market to a savvy investor who can see the profit potential in a house or neighborhood in the years to come.

The year 2008 brought a lot of uncertainty and apprehension to the real estate market. To some extent, those feelings remain as investors try to figure out their next move. Thankfully, with time to revaluate the situation of a sluggish economy and bad real estate market, many savvy investors are beginning to see the profit potential that lies ahead, thus reentering the real estate market. With a market that seems a long way off from rallying, many would-be investors are wondering if there is any hope in real estate these days. The answer is a resounding yes. Now is not just a good time to jump headlong into emerging markets — it is the best time. There are fortunes to be made in the coming years: You just have to know how to play the game.

Can you walk away from the real estate crash a winner? Are you one of the few with the guts to start buying while everyone else is selling? Do you really have what it takes to become a real estate mogul? Not every personality is right for the job. You have to be quick. You have to be smart. You have to savvy, and you have to have nerves of steel. Investing in emerging markets is definitely not for the faint of heart. Of course, striking it rich with real estate is not easy, and it is not guaranteed — especially in this climate. A few years ago, novice investors could enter the market almost guaranteed a profit, no matter how many stupid mistakes they made. That is no longer the case. One bad decision these days and you could end up broke. Still, those who take the time to learn the emerging markets game can — and likely will — turn a profit.

If you are looking for the next big deal, then it is time you learn exactly what you need to know to find profitable real estate investment opportunities in emerging markets. There are a lot of properties for sale these days, and while there are great deals to be had, too many novice investors will waste money on properties with little hope for success — not every property is equal when it comes to its profit potential. Because we have seen what most expects dub as rock bottom, the fact is that just about any house or condo will increase in value in the coming years. But why settle for a $10,000, or even a $25,000, return on your investment when you could double, triple, or even quadruple your profits? If you are smart enough to recognize each property's true profit potential and choose areas to invest in, you are almost guaranteed to skyrocket in value once the market rebounds. The real estate market has changed a lot, and the only investors who will walk away with cash-stuffed pockets are going to be those who learn exactly how to spot the real jewels among a lot of plain old clearance items. The goal of this book is not to show you how to make money in emerging markets: It is to show you how to make a lot of money.

So, how do you get started? *The Complete Guide to Locating and Profiting from Emerging Real Estate Markets* will teach you everything you need to know to strike it rich in emerging markets. The guide will not only show you how to find a great property, but it will show you how to finance it without using your own funds and how to use it to make money while the market remains soft. The big sale is not going to come for months, or even years, so it is important to know exactly how to make your emerging market investments work for you in the meantime. Ready to get started learning the best ways to invest in emerging markets?

SECTION I:

Getting In on the Ground Floor

There is no other way to starting investing in real estate than by hitting the ground running and building your way up to the top. You first need to understand which real estate markets are poised for success. When you have learned the mystery behind emerging markets, you will need to time your entrance perfectly in accordance to the market cycles, and learning how to read other people's panic in a downtrend is key to ensuring your money is well invested.

Chapter 1

An In-depth Look at Emerging Markets

Knowing the proper way to invest in emerging real estate markets is not always easy, especially for a newcomer. That is why it is important to know the answers to the five main questions new investors should ask themselves before looking at their first property.

What are Emerging Markets, and Why are They Lucrative?

If there is one mistake novice real estate investors make, it is only investing in their backyard. Not every neighborhood is poised for making the bigger profits available in emerging markets investing, and unless you are lucky enough to live in the middle of one of these up-and-coming neighborhoods, not expanding your real estate search could limit your profit potential. You must learn to expand your search.

The second mistake is not having a clear idea of what an emerging market is (and is not). Emerging markets are more than neighborhoods that are becoming more popular, although that is one indicator that an emerging market is beginning to come of age in a certain area. A true emerging market is one that is pegged to substantially increase in value in the near future due to a series of market indicators created by sudden profit-generating change.

The key to getting in on the ground floor of these value-busting markets is to recognize what neighborhood changes. When you are reviewing properties for the profit potential, you need to think about the surrounding area. Has it "arrived" yet? If not, why not? If you keenly scrutinize several market indicators and notice a trend toward sustained growth, than by all means jump into this market before anyone else notices. Getting in on the ground floor means just that: buying before everyone else does, and there are a lot of things to look for when scouting out solid investment opportunities.

Location

You have heard it a thousand times: When it comes to real estate, it is all about location, location, location. The location of a property may be important when it comes to selling any type of real estate, but it is *everything* when it comes to investing in emerging markets. Without the right location, a market cannot "emerge." In the past, emerging markets have traditionally been located outside of big cities or on the waterfront. While these areas are still considered good investment opportunities, there are a lot of new emerging markets hot spots opening up thanks to the foreclosure crisis.

For instance, take the suburban sprawl found outside of Philadelphia on the east coast over the last decade. Trying to escape the hustle and bustle of the city (not to mention the crime rate, taxes, and poor school system), many families opted to move north and east due to the excellent infrastructure that area offered. As land became scarce in those coastal areas and prices soared, up-and-coming professionals began to look farther west to build their homes. This caused a major influx of people in the late 1990s to the western Philadelphia suburbs, where there was more room to grow. Within just a few short years, houses in that area doubled and even tripled in price; a new house built in 1999 for a mere $175,000 was being sold for $350,000 just four years later. That was an emerging market that left early investors making hundreds of thousands of dollars in a relatively short time. Some of the leading indicators that foretold the sudden real estate boom in this market were:

- Increase in city taxes
- Poor city schools
- Increase in area jobs
- Population growth in the immediate suburbs
- Few newer homes available throughout the region
- Need for expansion throughout the area
- Land availability in the western suburbs (farms were quickly being turned into housing developments)

To spot an emerging market, watch in and around major cities for this same type of activity. Today, however, the trend is turning. With real estate taxes rising in the suburbs, little public transportation available into the city (and gas prices continuing to skyrocket), and few starter homes available in the suburbs, many young, single professionals and newly married couples are now heading away from the higher-priced suburbs for the fun, entertainment, and price of city dwelling. It might be hard to believe, but in some places, it is cheaper to live within the city limits rather than outside of it. Could there be a new emerging market looming in? Possibly.

If you think that Philadelphia is the only city to see this type of sprawl, look around. Cities young and old alike go through these sorts of fluctuating popularities. One generation cannot imagine living anywhere but in the midst of the city while the next strives to move outward into the calmer realms of the suburbs. What is important is to notice trends in the making in order to spot the next emerging market, wherever it may be.

Price

The price of homes can also signal an emerging market in the making. When it comes to price, you want to watch for two things:

1. A cheaper price tag on most homes than in the surrounding area
2. A sudden (but sustained) spike in price for the area

This may seem a bit confusing at first. After all, how can houses in an area suddenly spike, yet remain low? They can (and will) in an emerging market. Just because a neighborhood is cheap does not mean that it is a good investment. Actually, a neighborhood that is too cheap may indicate problems an investor will want to steer clear of. There may be reasons why property is selling so cheaply, such as a rough neighborhood, and it is your job to find out if those reasons will impact your ability to sell later for the price you want and need. But, if you are lucky enough to notice an inexpensive neighborhood and suddenly see more movement in housing prices, as well as a new type of homeowner moving in, it may indicate an up-and-coming area. People are drawn to an area for many reasons, but the main one is the mob mentality. This says that if everyone else thinks an area is great, it probably is. If you notice a trend that indicates a certain type of homeowner is moving into an area and you also see positive changes in the neighborhood and higher sales prices, it may be time to jump into this market. Popularity can and does affect pricing, so be on the lookout for neighborhoods that are showing growth. The temperature of the market is rising and the earlier you can get in on the ground floor, the more money you are apt to make.

Using price as a market indicator these days can be a bit trickier, however, considering that many areas have lost value in recent months. Just because it begins to rebound does not mean the market is truly emerging; it may just mean that it is recouping some of what it has lost.

Popularity

There is no use in buying an investment property in an area no one likes, no matter how cheap you can buy it. Look for popularity trends when scouting out potential markets. Check for an overabundance of for-sale signs in the neighborhood; if there seems to be too many, look into why. Could it be that the area is simply undesirable? Unless you can find evidence of change in the near future, then buying in an unpopular area may not be a good idea.

However, if you have done your research and found that any of the following are true, then investing in homes here may be a solid investment strategy:

- The school district is working hard to improve student test scores and improve their curriculum choices

- The school district or town has just landed a grant to build a new multi-million dollar facility

- Some new business initiative is being unveiled in the next few months that should bring more high-paying jobs to the area

- The arts community has pegged the surrounding area as its new place of operation

Be sure to consider why a place is becoming popular and if that trend is sustaining or at least if it will hold long enough for you to turn a tidy profit.

Which Neighborhoods are Poised for Profit Potential?

There is a lot more involved in spotting an emerging market than finding some cheap properties in a nice neighborhood. To make the most money from your investment, you must be able to spot up-and-coming neighborhoods before anyone else. This, of course, takes a keen eye and the ability to read a neighborhood.

Reading an area correctly requires some basic skills and an understanding of what it offers to draw in homeowners. The first thing to watch out for is that all of the amenities that make an area desirable are either currently in place or are in the process of being put in place. For instance, a small town that no one gave a second glance to for decades may suddenly come into its own if a developer suddenly puts a casino there, a large park area is added, or desirable shops are opened up. All of these things are "people attracters" and can signal that an area is about to get noticed.

Iowa is a great example of how this can work to create interest in an area. In a press release issued by the Iowa Department of Cultural Affairs, a new term called creative economy was explained, which outlined how a workforce can actually locate to a small town like the ones found sprinkled throughout the state "based on its cultural environment as well as job offerings." According to Dr. Richard Florida, who spoke at an

Iowa Cultural Affairs Conference in 2003, "creative people like indigenous street-level culture — a teeming blend of cafes, sidewalk musicians, and small galleries and bistros. They are drawn to places where outdoor activities are prevalent."

Investors who are smart enough to keep an eye out for areas offering this unique blend of culture and activities are well poised to spot the next emerging market. Once an area becomes desirable, the demand for housing increases, which shoots up property values. Many investors wait until prices begin to inch up before investing. While they will likely be able to make some money being safe, those who have the foresight to predict desirability in an area and buy into it while prices are still very low can walk away with hundreds of thousands in profits once an area becomes hot. When reading a neighborhood for future desirability, it is important to understand which trends signal growth.

Trends ensuring property value increases

Desirability by certain buying groups: Certain types of people want to buy homes in certain areas. For instance, many baby boomers are looking to retire in warmer climates, giving some southern states an open market. Of course, just because 50- or 60-year-olds want to move somewhere devoid of snow, sleet, and rain does not mean they will buy a home just anywhere. They will also be looking for senior-type amenities: Good healthcare, quiet residential areas, transportation, recreational opportunities, theaters, shopping, and a solid religious life. Find a neighborhood or town that offers everything a senior is looking for and the odds are good it is an emerging market worth a second glance.

While the baby boomer generation may be looking at higher-end, amenity-filled areas, their children (the 20- to 30-something-year-olds) are looking for more reasonably priced first homes. Since this demographic is generally fairly new to the workforce and may include young families, they have less to spend on housing and are looking for more family-friendly areas that feature larger bedrooms, backyards, and friendly streets that are chockfull of good parks, restaurants, children's activities, and top-notch schools.

The third buying group wielding a lot of power these days is immigrants. Although they are generally looking for more reasonably priced homes, this demographic is eager to own their own piece of the American dream, and are therefore creating emerging markets in areas where people from different nationalities may be naturally clumping together. For instance, Miami has a large Hispanic community, while California houses a large segment of the Asian community. Every large city has ethnic neighborhoods. These are a good place to begin your search. Keep a keen watch on immigration patterns within big cities and surrounding areas to spot new emerging markets erupting through increased immigration.

The area's educational system: One of the main priorities for most families these days is finding an excellent school system for their children. An investor who carefully investigates the school systems within a possible market may find them unable to unload their investment property easily. Parents want good (and safe) schools for their children. Many will not even consider purchasing a home in an area that does not offer quality educational choices. The best place to learn about a school district is on its official Web site. Here, you can learn about their national testing scores, the curriculum options they offer, the awards their staff and students are receiving, building projects, and special programs. Look for anything that shows improvements in individual neighborhood schools, as well as the district as a whole.

Affordability: An area does not have to be cheap to become an emerging market. Some higher-priced neighborhoods have seen drastic increases in value over the years for other reasons. For instance, an improvement in public transportation options may make an already desirable area a real hot spot for buyers. Sometimes something as simple as more shopping venues can increase an area's popularity. But it is smart to consider cost when evaluating a new market. A neighborhood that is already priced out is not likely to bring in much of a profit anytime soon. There is another thing to consider when looking at a neighborhood's affordability. Maybe the houses are fairly inexpensive but the local taxes are not, or vice versa. Higher-priced neighborhoods with lower taxes may be appealing to buyers who want more house for their money. On the other hand, if a buyer finds a home he or she can afford but realizes the taxes are too expensive, he or she may opt out of the sale. There really is no specific price point to look for when investing in emerging markets. What makes a property a good investment opportunity is not its asking price per se; it is rather the potential to command a much higher price when it comes time to sell. When it comes to emerging markets investment, a 25–50 percent (or more) return is usually desirable.

Transportation: Another important factor that can hold an emerging market back is transportation availability. Some areas will never become an emerging market simply because the infrastructure of the roads cannot handle an influx of people. There are reasons why rural areas remain that way: No one can get to work. Sure, housing may be affordable 60–90 minutes out of the city, but when a potential home buyer begins to factor in the time and cost of driving an hour or more to work every morning and the same back home at night, that cheaper house may quickly lose its appeal. Unless there are other factors to consider, like a solid public transportation option, this may be an area that yields little, if any, profit.

Consider this scenario: You, as an investor, have found a charming town with plenty of land for new housing. You notice local farms being snatched up by developers and wonder why. You hear a rumor and decide to check it out. A trip to the state capital yields some interesting information: A plan to expand the state's train system is in the works, which will connect this tiny little town with a major city that is a mere 30 miles away. While driving into the city would take near 90 minutes on these rural roads, a speed rail line would shorten that trip to just 25 minutes. You look further and notice the area sports one of the state's top five school districts, with a graduation rate of 97 percent and a college-bound rate of 92 percent. Plus, property taxes are currently 25 percent below other local neighborhoods. Is this an emerging market? You bet it is. You would be crazy not to start snatching up available property.

Jobs: The job market is another key factor in determining the probability that an area is on its way to becoming an emerging market. People need jobs to qualify for mortgages, so unless the employment outlook is good in an area, the odds are it may remain unknown for quite awhile. However, if you discover that a new factory will be opening soon, several businesses are expanding, or a new multi-building complex is going up in town, than you may want to take a closer look.

Local amenities: People love an area that offers a variety of things to do and places to visit. An area devoid of any type of recreational activities will be hard-pressed to draw in the large numbers of buyers that makes a market an emerging one. Some things to watch for that may signal future growth include:

- Shopping areas (either general, like an outlet mall, or very specific, as in art galleries)

- Museums

- Sporting venues

- Music offerings

- Theaters

- Parks

- Outdoor recreation areas (camping, skiing, fishing, boating, or golfing)

- Other attractions (amusement parks, skiing resorts, gaming parlors)

Population growth: Regardless of the reason behind it, any area that is experiencing a large influx of people is likely on its way to becoming an emerging market. As population increases, so will the need for housing, thereby raising current values (and prices).

Considering local market indicators

Taking notice of certain areas on the cusp of value increase is just the first step to predicting which neighborhoods will become emerging markets in the near future. There is still more work to be completed before you (or any investor for that matter) can safely say that an area is worthy of your investment. Here are a few things to consider when evaluating an area or neighborhood for emerging market status:

How many homes have sold recently?

Sales statistics can be a good indicator that an area is becoming more popular. Although a seasonal spike may not warrant much interest, a steady increase in sales over a period of a few months may be a sign that interest in an area is growing. Be careful not to buy during its peak, though. As soon as you notice any type of slowdown in housing sales, get out: This may be the first sign of saturation. You are not necessarily looking for high sales volume at this point. What you are looking for is a steady increase in the movement of properties, which may indicate increased interest — and the possibility of increased value in the months to come. There are a variety of ways to keep an eye on what the housing market is doing in a given area. To check sales trends in a specific area, you can contact the local tax office, office of deeds, local real estate agents, MLS listings, or even the sales records in the local newspaper.

How many properties are currently listed?

A lot of homes on the market at any given point can indicate two things:

1. The area is more popular and current owners want to sell to make big profits

2. The area is becoming more undesirable and the current homeowners want out

Since one of these scenarios is very good for an emerging markets investor and the other is not, it is important to figure out the exact reason why a large number of homes may suddenly be for sale in an area. One of the best ways to track the popularity of an area is to take a look at how many months it will take a property to sell. Most real estate experts agree that anything below 5 ½ months worth of supply is good for sellers and anything above 6 ½ months worth of supply is not good for sellers. Why? Because it will take you at least that long (and probably longer) to sell your property. Too many months between listing and a sale is cause for concern. To obtain this information, contact the National Association of Realtors (**www.Realtor. org**), which tracks supply and demand for specific areas.

How long is it currently taking to sell homes in that area?

Another key indicator for finding emerging markets is the number of days most homes are on the market before a sale is made. If a home is on the market for 120 days or more, it is an indicator that housing sales are slow. Anything under 60 days, however, is a sure sign of popularity in an area. Again, an emerging market will show signs of shorter sales times, but not necessarily quick ones. For instance if the average home was on the market for 100 days a year ago but only 60 days four months ago and 32 days now, you could assume that interest is growing. Be wary though. Some real estate professionals consider the number of days a house is on the market to be from the day of listing to the day of an offer; others consider it to be the first day that a house is listed until the day of closing. This can have a dramatic effect on statistics, so watch for overall trends and not just the number of days.

How many foreclosures are in the area?

With reports indicating as many as 2.8 million U.S. foreclosures in 2009 alone — this was a 21 percent increase from 2008 — this can be a tricky indicator to evaluate. In a normal market, too many foreclosures in an area may be a sign that an area is becoming depressed with dropping property values. In today's market, however, a larger-than-normal number of foreclosures does not necessarily indicate a troubled neighborhood. It could simply be a sign of the times, in which case it might offer some good investment opportunities.

The best thing to do if you notice more than a few foreclosures in a single area is to look at some other criteria and trends discussed to determine if it is a negative or positive sign for investment possibilities. For instance, if a local factory shut down and a large portion of the population lost their jobs but you hear of another factory or business moving in, the odds are the neighborhood will survive, and the market will eventually right itself (the sign of an emerging market). However, if all the businesses are closing down and no others seem interested in moving in, then the neighborhood may be on a downswing.

How many new construction permits are being issued?

If there is any one group of people who are tuned into an area's emerging markets profit potential, it is developers. They are generally right when it comes to spotting trends, since their business depends on it. They also spend countless hours and amounts of money doing the right kinds of research in upcoming areas, and tend to invest widely in places they believe offer a good prospect for profits.

Watch construction permit issuances carefully to determine if developer interest is rising. A steady increase in new permit requests is a good sign that a neighborhood is about to boom. This could be an early signal that other factors will soon be influencing real estate values in a specific area. Another benefit to keeping a careful eye on the number of construction permits being issued is the fact they will slow down well before housing sales hit their peak. Since it takes so long for a housing development to be built, developers tend to scale back months (or even a few years) before the actual market hits a downslide. This can be good news for a savvy investor who takes heed and begins to sell off their investment properties before the market becomes saturated and prices begin to tumble.

Which Investment Strategy is Best?

There are four main types of emerging markets to invest in: new construction, residential properties, condominiums, and commercial real estate. The way you handle your entire business hinges on figuring out which types of property you are most interested in buying, maintaining, and selling.

The residential market

Smaller residential properties are great places to learn the ropes of investing in emerging markets. Why? First, they are usually cheaper to purchase than, say, large-scale commercial properties. Second, they are much easier to manage, mainly because of their size. Remember, a quick resale is out of the question in today's market, so finding properties that you can make money on (and can handle) while you wait for the market to rebound is essential to your overall success. So, what types of residential properties should you be looking for? Here are a few places to consider and why they may be a good investment of your time and money:

The single-family home: From 1995 to 2005, the price of a single-family home in most of the United States doubled in price. That left many investors out in the cold when it came to renting these units, since it suddenly became cheaper to own a home than to rent one. Luckily for investors, things have changed. Renting is now the cheaper and easier option for many people when it comes to getting the house they want. The main reason, of course, is the fact that so many people have taken a major hit to their credit rating due to foreclosing their house or a job loss and no longer qualify for a mortgage. Left without a home of their own, they are forced to rent. This gives investors the opportunity to offer quality housing to many dependable families while waiting for the tide to turn. Add the fact that many banks are now selling off their foreclosure inventory for pennies on the dollar, and buying single-family dwellings to rent is suddenly a preferred investment opportunity among emerging markets gurus.

Duplexes: Before the recent housing crash, homeownership skyrocketed from the mid-1990s. By the time the real estate bubble burst in 2008, more than 69 percent of Americans were homeowners. That left a lot of one- to four-unit duplexes unable to find renters. This caused the prices for these buildings to plummet. Smart investors began to buy, knowing full well that every real estate cycle reverses itself and that rental properties would once again experience an upsurge. Eventually, housing prices would become so high that younger buyers with less income and older buyers on fixed incomes would be forced to rent. Watch for these types of trends when looking for rental investment opportunities. Look at the area's demographics to see if investing in smaller rentals is a good idea. Duplexes are usually sought after by small families with one or two children and by young couples who do not want to be an apartment complex.

Apartment complexes: Small apartment complexes can be a great investment in areas with a large young adult population — think about a city with a nearby college or university, or an area where single-family dwellings are at a premium. Larger than a duplex, which features less than five units, apartment complexes can range from 5–100 units. Be sure to consider the cost of handling such a large endeavor, both physically and financially. Becoming a landlord to so many tenants is not for everyone, so you should understand your responsibilities before you decide to buy this type of investment property. *You will learn more about being a landlord in Chapter 10.*

Vacation homes and rentals: If you are lucky and smart enough to be able to predict the next top vacation area, than you can make a fortune buying modest to high-end vacation homes. It does not matter whether you buy vacation proper-ties to resell or to rent out; the opportunity for profits is ripe in the right areas. As is the case in other emerging markets, you should look for trends that may be indicating an area is about to boom, such as famous people who frequent the area, new attractions cropping up, a surge in vacation-style shopping, or an influx in tourists.

Condominiums

Condominiums (condos) have grown in popularity in the last 10–15 years, according to reports published by the National Association of Home Builders (NAHB) and for good reason. They are a great investment for a larger number of people. Sin-gle homeowners love them because they offer the opportunity to own a home without all the work. Since most of the main-tenance is covered under the condo agreement, the owner is free to enjoy homeownership without the hassle of mowing the yard, shoveling snow, and fixing the plumbing.

Did You Know:

In 2004, condominiums accounted for more than a quarter of all multifamily construction in the United States, according to the National Association of Home Builders.

Young married couples love to both rent and buy condominiums because they are affordable. Plus, they are a good way to get their feet wet in the homeownership game. They offer the ability to have a practically full-sized house with no maintenance worries. The biggest downsize to condo living is the fact that many people feel as if they are still in an apartment setting (albeit a larger apartment). Several units are housed together through hallways, although some units offer separate outside entrances. Again, with little maintenance to worry about, newly married adults have the freedom to learn a bit about what a home needs before investing their time and money in a single-family dwelling. Baby boomers enjoy condo living for many of the same reasons as the other demographic groups; plus, they often cite location and size as major factors in choosing them.

Available from the small 700-square-foot home to the large 3,000-square-foot and beyond, condo size is only limited to the needs and interests of an area. Plus, many condos are located in thriving metropolitan areas, on golf courses, or on the waterfront, making them more desirable for older folks looking for a place to relax and have fun in their retirement years. Although most families prefer single dwellings not connected with a homeowners association (due to the restrictions many of these associations place on living there and the absence of common kid-friendly services and amenities), just about every other demographic group is drawn to this communal living arrangement, which makes condominiums a solid resource for investors.

Commercial real estate

With so much money at stake (usually millions) in the harrowing adventure, it takes a special knack, not to mention a lot of know-how, investing in commercial real estate. If you do not understand the nuances of commercial real estate, you can quickly lose a lot of money. Investing in emerging markets in this realm really is for advanced investors only. Still, we will discuss the basics to give the newbie investor something to strive for.

The first thing to consider is the type of commercial real estate you might be interested in. You can either purchase a ready-made business complex, shopping center, strip mall, or continue to lease each individual office or store; you can renovate an existing building such as an old factory or train depot, turning it into a one-of-a-kind office attraction; or you can build a new complex from scratch. Whatever strategy you choose, odds are you will face a lot of obstacles. Some of the most common obstacles commercial real estate investors face include:

- **Finding financial backers.** It is not always easy to find other investors willing to sink hundreds of thousands (or even millions) of dollars into a project that will likely not generate a quick profit. Commercial real estate is usually a long-term investment. Houses are bought to be sold, while commercial holdings are purchased to rent; thus, making money for years or even decades.

- **Locating solid properties.** Finding an emerging area is usually much easier than locating the right property within that area for a large-scale project. Why? Because most emerging areas do not have ready-made complexes available to renovate for a larger-scale project, but they often have land parcels available that can be used to build exactly what you want and need.

- **Dealing with zoning/building restrictions.** Many new investors make the mistake of thinking that investing in a small town will be easier than larger metropolitan areas because of zone and building codes. Nothing could be further form the truth. In most cases, smaller towns take a more hands-on approach than cities. Not only do they often have more building restrictions, they are less likely to approve variances to allow developers to bypass laws already in place.

- **Managing large projects.** Unless you have a large skill set and a lot of experience, managing a large-scale commercial project can be difficult.

- **Handling ongoing needs.** Buying commercial real estate and getting it leased is only the first step to commercial investing. Your property also needs to be managed for the long-term. If you are not qualified to handle the day-to-day operations, then you should find someone who can or you risk your investment.

New construction

The media may be touting a halt to new construction these days, but there are still plenty of ways for a smart investor to make money in this area. *Chapter 4 offers more detail on new construction opportunities.* Some of the basics, however, are covered here.

New construction can be very profitable, especially when an emerging market specialist can snag a new development during the pre-building stage, which is usually after all of the plans have been made and approved, but before actual construction begins. When the economy is good, the best way to make money in new construction is to pre-buy at rock bottom prices before the developer ever breaks ground. Oftentimes, builders sell off a few sites early at a discount to raise quick capital. If purchased in the right area and at the right time, this can garner a fairly easy (and quick) turnover of profits, with investors getting back two to three times their initial investment in a matter of months. Now, in a poor economy and real estate market, developers may be struggling to stay afloat. This leaves them in need of cash, and what better way to make some much-needed cash than to sell off either partly finished projects or projects that have not even been started yet?

An emerging markets investor who sees the potential for future profits can often buy up a developer's leftovers, that last property or two in a development that has not sold, for a fraction of the property's real worth. Even if no homes have been built on the parcel yet, the odds are good that all of the building approvals and costly road evaluations have been completed, and even in-ground sewer and electrical lines have been laid. That means less work and cost for you in the future. When the time comes, you can simply hire a new contractor to build the houses you need and sell them at a hefty profit. However, partially finished buildings can be a little trickier to handle. Some investors simply tear down partially constructed buildings and wait for the market to turn around before rebuilding, while others opt to finish the work that has already been started. Either strategy can work; whichever you take depends on your expertise, comfort level, and amount of financing available.

How Do I Choose Between Multiple Potential Properties?

Once you have decided what type of property to invest in and have established an area that is ripe for growth, the next step is looking for potential profit makers. More than likely, you will come across more than one property you would like to invest in. So, how do you choose between two great deals? There are five must-haves that every property you buy must include.

1. **The right price:** When considering a potential property, be sure to look for bargain basement-priced properties only. Of course, if there is only a few thousands dollars difference between two properties, and the higher-priced home needs much less work or is located in a better neighborhood, you will want to consider the higher-priced one that is better positioned to sell. But, if you are considering two properties that are worlds apart in respect to price, yet seem equal in other areas, you want to choose the cheaper one. Paying well below the actual property value is essential when investing in emerging markets. Otherwise, you may be stuck holding a house too long and make very little profit in the final sale.

2. **The ability to increase in value:** Unless you have reasons to believe a particular property will increase in

value 20, 30, or 50 percent by the time you want to sell, then it probably is not a keen investment opportunity. Some other things that may indicate a valuation change are improvements in neighborhoods, renovation or remodeling, an increase in other properties within the local area, or some other circumstance that is unique to that particular house or neighborhood, such as new job opportunities, new entertainment venues, or an increase in educational opportunities.

3. **The ability for the property to pay for itself during holding:** Carrying costs on any property can be hefty: Try paying those costs on several investment properties with no end in sight. Do not consider buying a property that does not offer an opportunity to pay for itself now, as well as later. If you find an investment property that can be easily rented during the holding period, then by all means put it on your maybe list. Renting is a fantastic way to pay your ongoing carrying costs, such as insurance, utilities, and taxes, while making a small profit to boot. When the time comes to sell, you will be ahead of the game with small monthly profits to add to your overall sales profit. Plus, your property will be cared for and lived in while you wait for the market to turn around. This can help to increase its value since potential buyers do not have to fear maintenance issues caused by neglect.

4. **A great location:** When it comes to real estate, there is nothing more important than location. Choose a perfect house in the wrong neighborhood and you will find it hard to sell. But, purchase a so-so property in a great neighborhood and you can do the improvements nec-

essary to make the house a real winner. If you consider location more important than either price or condition when looking for real estate to invest in, you will come out on the winning side of every deal.

5. **The ability to meet the need of several demographics groups:** One of the biggest mistakes new investors make is choosing properties based on the needs of one demographic group. For instance, they may buy a property that suits a single professional well, but not a retiree or a couple. That investor has just made the job of selling that property much harder. It may be a good idea to have a specific target group in mind when buying investment properties, but try your best not to limit a property's availability to one specific demographic group.

For instance, let us say that you have found a property in an up-and-coming neighborhood for single professionals. Houses are small in the region, which is good considering your target group. Now, assume you find two properties: one a second-floor condo featuring every upgrade available on the market and the other a ranch-style single that needs a bit of renovating for about the same price. Although the prices are compatible, the single may be a better choice. Why? Right now the area is attracting mostly single professionals, but what happens when newly married couples or even a few younger retirees start to move in? That second floor condo may not seem as appealing to a group who does not like communal living or is not thrilled about dragging grocery bags up four flights of stairs. Plus, a family can make a single dwelling (even a small one) better than the fancier condo, if necessary. With a few upgrades and a bit of work, you can add the amenities of the condo to the single-family home and open up your market possibilities to a whole host of new buyers. Moreover, a single dwelling is often easier to rent during a down market.

Consider carefully who might be interested in each investment property. If the properties do not appeal to several different buying groups, than consider how difficult making a sale will be.

Will this Property Make Money?

You are in emerging markets to make money. The bottom line to any investment is making money, and you will learn how to determine the profit potential of a specific property throughout the rest of the book. For now, the most important thing to ask yourself is how much money you will feel satisfied making on each property you consider buying, rather than whether the property can meet those profit expectations. No one knows for sure exactly how much he or she will walk away with once an investment property has been sold, but a knowledgeable investor should be able to determine if a certain property can at least meet his or her absolute bottom line for profit. If you think it may be difficult to make what you want and need on a certain property, then reconsider the purchase. There are plenty of great opportunities in emerging markets these days, so do not settle for a property that may make some money when you can find one that will make you lots of money.

Once you have successfully asked and answered these five basic questions, it is time to learn more about real estate cycles and how to successfully time a prosperous emerging markets purchase.

CASE STUDY: LONG-TERM POTENTIAL IS THE KEY TO SUCCESS

Ryan Hinricher,
founder of Investor Nation
www.investornation.com

When investor Ryan Hinricher began investing in real estate in 2000, the market was thriving and making money. Purchasing a home was simple, with no money down loan options readily available and home prices on the upward swing. Fast-forward ten years, and the market is in a very different condition, but Hinricher is still able to make it work for him and be successful as a real estate investor.

Hinricher concedes that people have become more conservative in their investments, staying away from speculative plays and concentrating more and more on real estate investments that actually pencil from the cash flow perspective. The strategies that once worked, especially those that depended on careless financing, are no longer working in our volatile economy. The smart investor will be looking for a new strategy for real estate investing that will be lucrative in the long run.

Investor Nation offers turnkey rental opportunities and has a clear idea of which markets will emerge stronger after this recession. It is not the typical, glamorous coastal areas that so many people were investing in during the height of the market. Rather, it is cities like Indianapolis, Birmingham, Charlotte, Memphis, Dallas, and Kansas City, along with other Southern and Midwestern towns that did not see the meteoric rise in prices witnessed in some states that will be the new fertile ground for investing. These areas did not see prices triple or quadruple as they did in California or New York, and will rebound better than areas that saw a huge inflation in price over a short period of time.

Emerging markets such as these are a great way for a new investor to get into real estate investment, thanks to easily affordable price points and a good return on the investment. Hinricher has been steadily building his portfolio with properties in these types of areas as rents have held steady and prices are well below market values due to high foreclosure rates. New investors may think that the traditional investment markets like Florida, Arizona, or California are a safe bet, but in this climate it is the less glamorous, but more stable city that will have the best long-term growth prospects.

A long-time investor and observer of market trends, Hinricher has good advice for a new investor — look for a Target. Really, if the big stores like The Home Depot, Lowe's Home Improvement, and Target are building in the area where you are considering investing, they have already determined that the area has promise. You can piggyback off their due-diligence, Hinricher reminds us. He also advises any investor, even a seasoned one, to focus on quality first. His ideal property has three bedrooms, two bathrooms, and a garage, which is what tenants and buyers are looking for. Hinricher is a good example of an experienced investor using emerging markets to his advantage.

Chapter 2

In Real Estate, Timing is Everything

When it comes to buying real estate, timing is everything. Buy too soon and you will be stuck with your investment (and its associated carrying costs) for a while; buy too late and you will short-change yourself of profits others are making. Learning how to time your purchases and your sales properly will ensure your success as an emerging market expert. But first, you must pinpoint what type of investor you are.

Types of Buyers

Understanding which type of buyer you are can not only help you save yourself from buying outside your comfort level, but it can also keep you from making costly mistakes. While each buying style presents itself with its own benefits and risks, one is not better than another, as you will soon see. The process you use is up to your own comfort level and experience. There are three main types of buyers:

1. **The low-point buyer:** A low-point buyer is someone who sees the market sliding and buys while prices are low, but before they have hit rock bottom. Not concerned that they may miss a few good deals, low-point buyers do not worry about losing a few thousands dollars to ensure they get the exact properties they want at a price they can afford — and ones that will make then a tidy sum when the market rebounds.

2. **The bottom buyer:** The bottom buyer, more commonly referred to as a contrarian buyer, is one who waits until the market has hit rock bottom to buy properties for much less than their actual value. Although these buyers tend to make more money on each individual property they invest in, they sometimes miss getting the property they want by waiting too long. Contrarian buying comes with its own risks, including getting stuck with the worst properties the market has to offer. For some investors, the ultra-low price at this stage of the real estate cycle is worth doing some major repairs or renovations to bring the best out on a property.

3. **The momentum buyer:** The momentum buyer, on the other hand, plays it much safer. This buyer waits until the market begins to rebound, and then looks for good investments. Although momentum buyers will pay much more for a particular property, they usually do not have to wait long for a sale or a profit. This can be a huge incentive for investors who either cannot or do not favor taking big risks.

What is the Real Estate Cycle?

Once you know what type of investor (or buyer) you are, you will be able to better time real estate cycles and when is best for you to begin looking for investment properties to purchase. But, what exactly is a real estate cycle? At its most basic level, a real estate cycle is the natural ebb and flow of the market. It goes up and it goes down. The real estate market is constantly on the move. Prices may inflate rapidly and unpredictably; they may also fall just as quickly and sometimes without much warning. Understanding this roller coaster ride of pricing and sales is the best and quickest way to make a profit in emerging markets.

Let us take a closer look at how real estate cycling can make it a buyer's or seller's market. California is a prime example of how current cycling has taken place. From about 1999 to early 2008, California experienced a sudden and dramatic rise in real estate. As more and more investors jumped onto the flipping bandwagon, taking ordinary or even devastated properties and turning them into high-priced homes in growing sought-after areas, real estate prices in many areas skyrocketed. As prices continued to rise, few people thought about when they would hit the ceiling and begin to fall again — except, of course, savvy real estate professionals who understood cycling. They knew the importance of watching for signs of a turnaround and unloaded their properties before anyone else noticed the downturn. Many others were not so lucky. Some, in fact, lost more than just their original investment. In most of these hard-hit areas, property owners saw their values plummet anywhere from 20–60 percent, leaving most owing more on their homes than they could sell them for.

There are typically four parts to a real estate cycle:

1. **The upward climb:** This is the time when prices are moving upward. The upward climb can happen at a slow and steady pace, or at a quick and unpredictable one.

2. **The plateau:** A time of stabilization, the plateau is a stoppage of price increases when prices remain relatively the same.

3. **The downward spiral:** This is the time when prices begin to drop. The downward spiral can happen very quickly, or it can take months or years of falling prices before this part of the cycles comes to an end.

4. **The bottom:** When a market bottoms out, it means the lowest price has been reached; the cycle has come to an end, and prices will begin their upward climb again. The biggest profits are usually experienced when buying at this time.

There is an old saying: What goes up must come down. This is especially true during a real estate cycle. Sometimes the fall is minimal and sometimes it is not. The key to making money in any type of real estate market is to know when to enter the cycle (preferably while it is down) and when to get out (while it is high and before the next downturn). Get greedy and you may lose more than you bargained for. Remember, there is no telling how long each phase of the cycle will last. Some are completed in a matter of months, while others take years to complete themselves. There is no way to say for certain how long a single cycle will take. All an investor can do is watch for the signs discussed in this book and make their own calculations using the information they have available. When and how to enter the market in each phase is solely up to you, your interests, your cash flow, and your comfort level.

The making of a real estate bubble

Not every downward cycle is a real estate bubble, although it may feel like that to investors on the losing end. A real estate bubble is more than a downturn in the market, which is part of real-life real estate cycling. A true real estate bubble occurs when housing prices inflate unnaturally and quickly. What may look like an emerging market taking place could, in fact, be a bubble waiting to burst.

A real estate cycle shows a slow, healthy climb in prices with an equally slow (and healthy) downturn in price, then back to a more normal pricing structure. During a real estate bubble, however, prices spike suddenly and can drop just as suddenly. A house worth $150,000 in June could be worth $320,000 by December and $110,000 by the following summer. The best way to gauge natural real estate cycling and a real estate bubble is to question if the sudden rise in price is reasonable. Real estate bubbles tend to offer unrealistic prices for no good reason. Anyone looking at the houses during a bubble would question such a hefty price tag during any other time. The only thing that keeps it going is a herd mentality that says the property is worth that price even though it is not. While a herd mentality keeps prices high for awhile, reality will hit and financing breaks down, buyers can no longer afford the prices, or they simply figure out how overpriced an area is and they stop buying. This sends prices tumbling, sometimes even farther below their original starting point.

The good news for investors is that the market will eventually correct itself, and if you buy while these properties are low, you will be able to make some money on them. The bad news is that a burst bubble can take a while to fix itself, and prices rarely make it back up toward their heyday.

Trends Affecting Real Estate Cycles

A lot of things can affect a real estate cycle, and there are the seven major trends to watch out for. Each on their own can affect housing prices, but when you notice these seven trends coming into play together, watch out: Big changes in the market are ahead.

Inflation

When we think of inflation we usually think, "Oh no, prices are going up." Fortunately, that is good news for real estate investors. Rising prices means more money in their (and your) pockets.

A moderate rise in inflation generally means that the price of housing will also rise. Too much inflation, however, can be bad for business. When inflation rose 10 percent during the 1970s, real estate prices dropped, noted especially when they bottomed out in 1973. How far depended on the area, but most people nationwide saw at least a 10–20 percent decrease in their property value. Why? The answer is simple: Average living expenses were rising faster than rent and house prices could. People could not afford to pay more for their housing and their day-to-day living expenses, so they stopped buying.

On the opposite spectrum is deflation, which is just as bad for the real estate market. During deflationary times, things get cheaper and cheaper, including materials for new houses. This leaves many consumers scrambling to build brand new homes in lieu of older ones that cost more. This trend then sends built home sales into a major slump, which eventually erodes their prices. Again, the seller (you) is on the losing end of the deal.

Timing Recommendation

- Less than 10 percent inflation can be handled without much risk of loss, so you can feel relatively safe in buying, selling, and holding at this stage of the real estate cycle.

- Inflation of more than 10 percent is a good time to hold or sell, since prices can be rather high at this stage.

- When deflation hits, it is time to sell. Prices are going to continue to drop, so get out while you still can. Buying too early in a deflationary cycle can cost you a bundle since you will be unlikely to sell or rent your property for the amount needed to cover your costs.

Interest rates

Interest rates can have a big impact on the real estate cycle, both on the local and national levels, and for good reason. The lower the interest rate, the more money people can borrow for housing purchases. This allows some lower- to middle-income buyers the chance to enter the housing market in the first place, while giving others more bucks to buy with. This is good news if you are on the buying or selling end. It is not good for those investing in rental properties since, in this part of the real estate cycle, more people are buying and less are renting. This can drive rents (and profits) down.

Timing Recommendation

- The lower the interest, the better chance you have of selling for a higher price.

- High interest rates are a bad time to buy since your own carrying costs and mortgage will also be high — even though sales prices are lower.

- Moderate interest rates between 5–10 percent are the best time to buy, sell, or hold. Basically, new investors should watch for these interest rates to make any moves at all.

Funding

Success usually breeds success. So, what does that mean for real estate? If investors are making money in emerging markets, they will have no trouble getting their hands on more funds to invest. But, if real estate is down, they may not be able to get the money they need to buy up new properties, no matter how good the deal.

In fall 2008, the banks stopped lending to everyone. This caused a serious problem for the real estate market. Even people with good credit and solid employment could not get a mortgage. The same was true for investors who saw a chance to buy great properties for pennies on the dollar. This lack of funding only exacerbated an already serious problem. Trying to ward off a real economic catastrophe, the U.S. Congress approved almost $1 trillion to help support the banks and get money moving again. This government aid (most commonly known as Troubled Asset Relief Program, or TARP, money) was aimed at giving lenders money to lend without the fear of nonpayment.

As we saw at the time, our nation's entire economic survival hinges on the ability for everyone to borrow money. This is especially true when it comes to the real estate market. Without the ability to obtain a mortgage, very few average Americans can buy a house, which sends the market into a tailspin. So, when funds stop flowing for whatever reason, the real estate cycle begins a new downturn.

Timing Recommendation

- When money is flowing into real estate, you want to buy or hold for the best deals, but it is time to sell when money begins to flow out of real estate.
- If you entered the cycle too late and prices have already begun to dip, hold onto your investment property until the cycle corrects itself.

The employment outlook

When employment prospects in an area look good, more people feel confident enough to invest in a home, but when jobs are lost, few people can afford to pay the mortgage they already have, let alone look for a new house. While the employment outlook is usually a local trend affecting only a certain area's real estate cycling, when job losses reach epidemic proportions, as has been the case of the recession beginning in late 2007, it affects the national real estate cycle. When national unemployment rates hit six percent or above, real estate all over the country may suffer. When it reaches double digits as it did in December 2009, people are afraid to invest in a 30-year mortgage, no matter how safe they think their job is.

In some ways, high unemployment may help the wealthy investor, enabling them to take advantage of others' disadvantage by buying properties on the cheap. Unfortunately, it also means that they will be forced to hold onto those properties for months or years until the job market in the area recovers and people not only have a chance to save down payment monies again, but feel confident that buying a house is once again a safe investment for themselves and their families.

Timing Recommendation

- Buy or hold onto property when the job outlook is good, but sell as soon as you see a decline in employment offerings.

Migration patterns

When people want to move into an area, housing prices soar due to high demand and low availability. This is called in-migration and causes a spike in the real estate cycle. When the opposite happens (out-migration), the real estate cycle turns downward once again, simply due to the fact that there are suddenly too many houses for sale with too few buyers bidding on them. This drives prices down. Of course, with real estate being so cyclical, the trend usually reverses itself with time.

Timing Recommendation

- Buying or holding while people are still coming into an area is usually pretty safe, but sell as soon as you begin to see any type of mass exodus in an area.

The path of progress

A local trend that affects the real estate cycles in specific areas, particularly in and around busy cities, is the path of progress; that is, what else is being built in the area that will affect its purpose, interest, and housing availability? The building of new roads, an airport, substantial shopping arenas, entertainment venues, and large office buildings or manufacturing plants are all considered paths of progress and can make an otherwise stagnant area jump to life, bringing in more jobs, more people, and more general interest.

Timing Recommendation

- Since the path of progress in most areas lasts for years, it can be easy to feel safe for too long. As long as building and immigration to an area remains strong, feel free to buy or hold.

- Watch for signs of oversaturation or a real estate bubble to avoid getting stuck with too many investment properties once the tide turns.

New construction availability

New construction can do one of two things to a real estate cycle:

1. It can shoot it upward due to a lack of availability (not enough new construction).

2. It can send it into a downward slide if there are too many new houses being built.

Keep a close eye on the number and types of new construction being built in an area. For instance, if most developers are constructing townhomes, the odds are good that 4,000-square-foot mini-mansions are not going to be in high demand. However, if the only things being built are upscale homes, more moderately priced (and sized) ones may not be a top priority for this neighborhood's buyers.

Another thing to watch out for is a sudden decrease in construction in a particular area, especially one that has been in a boom. As we already discussed, new construction tends to slow down or come to a complete halt a few months before the general real estate market in a particular area, so keep a close eye on what those developers are doing to better gauge where you are in the current cycle and what you should do about it.

Chapter 3

Panic Can Be a Good Thing

A lot of people are panicky these days when it comes to real estate. Homeowners who have watched the equity in their homes dry up are eager to strike a deal before they lose even more. Those facing foreclosure are agreeing to just about anything to salvage at least some of their credit rating, and banks overloaded with real estate owned (REO) properties are selling great inventory for pennies on the dollar just to free themselves from burdening taxes and maintenance costs. Panic is thick and that is good news for the savvy investor willing to wait awhile to cash in on their first outlay of money. This is the time to position yourself (and your investments) to make a fortune when things finally turn around. This downward spiral will not last forever, and those taking a risk today will find themselves in the winner's circle when the dust clears.

The Power of Contrarian Timing

In the last chapter, we talked briefly about buying when the market has hit rock bottom. While this may have made perfect sense earlier, consider this: Contrarian timing involves buying when there is panic in the air — buying when everyone else is selling. At this point in the cycle, there have been others who have tried to invest wisely, believing that the market was about to rebound, only to discover that they lost a lot of money. Contrarian buying is not easy, and it is not a sure thing. Project poorly and you will lose a lot of money. But know your market and be willing to take a risk buying at a time when everyone else is afraid, and you can reap big rewards.

The most important obstacle to watch out for is a market that continues to fall. Predicting when the bottom has been hit can be difficult, especially for someone new to real estate. So be careful and take advantage of any seasoned advice you can find, including the advice found in this book. Learning how to predict this stage of a real estate cycle takes practice. Unfortunately, most amateur investors do not fully understand it until they have lived through at least one complete cycle and have made some mistakes along the way. One of the best things you can do until you learn how to spot changes in the real estate atmosphere yourself is to watch other investors carefully, looking for the subtle signs that they are about to make a move — then jump in with momentum as your guide.

Another thing to watch out for are permanent trends that could affect a real estate market beyond its ability to rebound. Yes, real estate is cyclical and a market that is down will likely rebound in the future, but there are exceptions. Right now, Michigan is in a terrible mess due to the national recession. So is California and Nevada. Since there is more at play regarding their economy than just a national recession, their housing market may not rebound as quickly as other parts of the country. For instance, until Michigan sees resurgence in manufacturing and their residents have jobs again, their real estate prices will stay low. California needs to get control of its budget before things can turn around there, and Nevada may have simply seen the peak of its real estate, at least until tourism picks back up again. Be sure to watch for signs of a more serious issue than natural cycling when looking for good real estate buy. A rebound is likely, but not guaranteed.

If you are a risk taker who finds it thrilling to try and figure out when a market has reached bottom, then you will want to be sure to follow some basic rules of contrarian timing.

1. Always Have a Plan

It is more important for contrarian buyers to have a plan. Now is not the time to buy blindly. Know exactly where you are in the real estate cycle and what you will do if things do not go as planned. Have enough cash reserves on hand to withstand a longer-than-expected turn around and be sure to think about all of the things that can go wrong. Some investors like to have at least twice the amount they think they will need, but most tack on 20 percent to their expected costs.

What will you do if renting is not an option? What will you do if a hurricane strikes and your property suddenly needs major improvements or repairs? Have a back-up plan for your back-up plan so that nothing leaves you scrambling to figure out an answer to an emergency. Trying to buy at the bottom of a cycle is risky and success depends on you having a plan to handle just about anything that might be thrown your way. Know what to expect and when to get out. Anticipating the worst can only result in the best. Things never go as badly as we imagine as long as we are realistic and prepare for the worst.

2. Always Have Enough Cash

If there is one thing you can count on when investing in real estate, it is that unexpected expenses will come up. Nothing is worse than making it almost to the end of a downward cycle and finding yourself without the cash to turn your gem into a priceless diamond to make the most money. Remember, when dealing in emerging markets, the goal is not to make money — it is too make a lot of money. Be sure to have enough funding in place to not only withstand your holding time, but to make the improvements necessary to sell at top prices once the market does rebound.

3. Show Some Patience

It can be hard in a long real estate spiral to remain positive, especially when you see your investment earnings dwindling right before your eyes. Now is not the time to get discouraged, but to remember why you went into emerging markets in the first place. Those with patience and a positive attitude will emerge profitable. Those who panic and run will lose more than their investment: They will lose an opportunity.

4. Be Realistic

You may be a great salesperson who can convince everyone else around you that the market is turning around and now is the time to buy, but be realistic. Know what signs to watch for and be careful not to fall for your own pitch. When flipping houses was at its peak, there were far too many people who believed it was a never-ending stream of opportunity. Those were the people who lost it all when the market screeched to a halt. Those who took the time to read the road signs along the journey saw what was ahead and veered off the course. They are the ones who survived the crash, and will likely be the ones who make a fortune in their return when the market rises. Never lose sight of what is really going on in the market no matter what the press and other investors are telling you. Listen to what the market is telling you, and you will not get stuck with a load of unsalable inventory.

A real profit booster

While there can be some real risks to trying to predict the bottom of a real estate cycle, contrarian timing is usually pretty safe. As long as you have enough time and money to get you through the climb upward again, buying at rock bottom prices gives you the absolute best chance at making a huge profit once the market rebounds. Buying high and selling a little higher can yield profits but not like contrarian buying can. Consider this: Would you rather buy a home for $150,000 and sell it for $175,000 three months later or buy a home for $85,000 and sell it for $210,000 18 months later? Your answer may be the first. If you are one of those people who need an instant payoff, than forget contrarian timing — it is not for you. But if you are a patient investor looking for the biggest profit payoff, than consider buying at the lowest point possible and waiting for higher prices to come your way.

Dangers of investing at the bottom

Remember: There are always risks to any type of investing, and with contrarian buying having huge potential for profit, there is also the biggest risk involved. Here are a few dangers to watch out for when considering buying at the bottom.

- **You may be going it alone:** It can be hard to find both lenders and investors to back up your investments when common sense says to stay away. Many contrarian buyers must finance their own projects or find a group of like-minded investors willing to take the risk and wait for the rewards.

- **Your timing may be off:** Buy too early in the cycle and you could lose everything. Even the savviest investor can wrongly predict the bottoming out of a market, only to discover too late that more losses were ahead. Unless you are financially prepared to weather the storm, you could put your investment at risk. Nothing is worse than buying too soon, losing your investment, and discovering months or years later that you were right all along as you watch others walk away with the profits that were earmarked for you. The same is true if you sell too early, even if you buy at the right time.

- **Not every market rebounds:** Most markets rise out of the ashes, but some do not. There have been times and places where the real estate market became so depressed it either never rebounded or took decades to climb back up. Most investors do not have the kind of time to roll a property over. Be sure to avoid this pitfall by learning and watching for the seven trends already discussed.

Also, take note of permanent changes that may be taking place in an area that would affect property sales for years to come.

Momentum Timing for the Thin-skinned

Momentum buyers are willing to risk a huge payoff for one that is smaller and more guaranteed. When you buy as the market begins to rebound, you let the momentum of the climb take the price of your house upward. That momentum, combined with any improvements you make, should result in a tidy profit. The key to making momentum buying work in your favor is the ability to recognize when housing prices have stabilized and are on their way toward an up again. You should watch for these important signs in a real estate cycle:

- **An improvement in the overall economy:** A sluggish or recessive economy hurts the real estate market, but when the economy begins to turn around, so does the housing market. Whether it is a local or national recession, watch for any improvements to indicate an upward swing in the real estate cycle.

- **Job growth:** In a depressed job market, there is no income to pay for mortgages. This leaves sellers with no buyers, which causes housing prices to fall. Any sign of job growth is a good indicator that housing prices will begin to stabilize and return to a more normal level.

- **Open lending and stable interest rates:** When lenders stop lending or make it harder to qualify for loans, real estate sales come to a screeching halt. Erratic interest rates can also scare off potential buyers. Once interest rates stabilize in a tough market and lenders begin offering loans again, the market usually bounces back rather quickly.

As is the case with any type of real estate investing scheme, there are risks to consider when using momentum buying.

- **Waiting too long to jump into the market:** It is not always easy to recognize the best time to begin buying in a momentum timing market. Wait too long and you will substantially reduce your profit potential. The best time to buy is as soon as you notice market prices stabilizing and inching upward.

- **Erratic cycles:** Momentum buying cycles can last as little as 18 months, which leaves little time to recognize it is happening and to take advantage of it. It could also last as long as several years, which means if you buy early, you will have to wait a while before seeing a return on your investment.

- **Holding too long:** If you buy at the right time but hold too long, you could miss the opportunity to make a tidy profit. If you wait until the cycle begins another downturn, you could lose out. Do not get greedy. Know how much you want to make on your property. When the market hits that level, sell.

The Importance of Building a Solid Business Team

If you thought you could look for investment properties on your own, decide which ones to buy, handle all aspects of the sale yourself, then handle those rentals all on your own, you are very wrong, especially if there is panic in the real estate market.

True, a small-time investor may be able to handle the acquisition, renovation, maintenance, and rental of a few smaller properties. However, if you are serious about investing in emerging markets, you will have to develop a core group of knowledgeable professionals to turn to when you do not know how to handle something or simply do not have the time to do it yourself. If you are going to succeed in the emerging markets industry, you will need a solid investing team comprised of the following knowledgeable players that can be responsible for individual aspects of your new investment business.

Buying and selling

Never underestimate the power of a great real estate broker. These are ones who know the area, understand real estate cycles, have a solid network of their own in containing new properties (including bank-owned properties and foreclosures), and are willing to go out of their way to find the right kind of deal for you. Not every real estate broker has the insight or connections to find great investment opportunities. You can save a lot of time and effort by finding one that will do the legwork for you.

In addition to your acquisitions broker, you may need to find a broker experienced in sales. Not every good acquisitions broker can or does sell properties to average homeowners. While finding good buys is important to your bottom line, so is being able to get the price you want in a timely manner once it is time to sell. Some things to look for in a sales broker are:

- The number of buyers their office currently has listed

- Their total number of sales last year compared to their total number of listings

- Their total sales income (how much they sold in dollars)

- The average sales price of the homes they sold

- The average length of time it took them to sell each of their listings

- The types of homes and buyers the agent specializes in

- Proper state licensing

- Someone who is a member of the National Association of Mortgage Brokers (NAMB) or the Mortgage Brokers Association (MBA)

- Someone who comes with plenty of referrals

Whether you hire an in-house agent to handle all of your buying and selling needs or you use commissioned real estate brokers from an established agency is really a matter of choice. While hiring in-house brokers can guarantee better service at times, it is usually more expensive and can cheat you out of a larger buyer's group to pull potential buyers from.

A good title company: It is a good idea to pay a little extra to have your own title company research each property you decide to buy to ensure the title is clear. Plus, hiring a title company to handle your searches can generate its own leads, since the people there may have a heads-up on other distressed properties that have not yet hit the market.

A quality home inspector: It is always a good idea to inspect any potential property carefully before making an offer. This is especially true for distressed properties that may have been neglected for a while by their previous owners. Most investors are not experienced enough to inspect a potential property themselves. This takes the trained eye of a person with firsthand knowledge of all major systems, like plumbing, heating, electrical, foundations, and roofing in order to spot potential problems. That is why hiring a qualified inspector is best. Ask these important questions when looking for a home inspector:

1. Are you certified, licensed, and insured? Since many areas do not require any type of formal education or experience to become a home inspector it is always best to use only those who have been certified by their local trade organization or municipality.

2. How long have you been working as an inspector?

3. What experience do you bring to the job? Many professional contractors become home inspectors when it is time to retire. Using an inspector with solid contracting experience will give you an idea as to realistic costs in fixing those problems and what the work will entail.

4. How many homes have you inspected in the last year? The more houses a person inspects, the better they get at spotting potential issues. Inspectors who do not work regularly may not have the experience you need.

5. May I check your references? Anyone who is not willing to give you the names and contact information of past clients may have something to hide.

Financing

Financing your investments is a complicated topic, so it is important to establish a qualified financing team to ensure success. This generally includes:

A lender: Without money, you cannot buy any property. This fact alone can make your lender the most important entity to your business survival, not to mention success. Get to know your lender well. Find out what they are looking for in the deals they will fund. If a specific lender wants you to contribute half down on each property, there is no point in continuing a relationship if you can only cover one-third of the purchase price.

Outside investors: In addition to a bank or other lending facility, you may want to consider looking for other investors to help front the money needed to buy and maintain your investment properties. These can include family, friends, or business associates that will help fund your projects in either a silent-partner manner or with more interest (and say) as to the way you run your business.

A good accountant: The laws regarding real estate investment and taxes are constantly changing. Without a knowledgeable accountant on your side, odds are you will unknowingly pay thousands more per year on taxes than you need to. Here are just a few of the other benefits of finding a tax-savvy accountant:

a. You will not have to worry about an IRS audit. Even if you are called in, your accountant will explain and handle everything.

b. You will not miss any allowable expenses, thus saving you money.

c. You will not have to handle any of the financial paperwork associated with your business on your own.

d. You will have someone else to help keep your expenses in line by reminding you when you go over budget.

A real estate attorney: A knowledgeable real estate attorney can come in handy when dealing with foreclosure purchases, tax lien purchases, and property auctions, as well as title searches and landlord disputes. In addition, their expertise can often save you thousands of dollars when dealing with municipality zoning requirements and building/renovation projects. For example: One investor solicited a real estate attorney who worked for one township while he was investing in another township. Although the attorney he hired did not have a conflict of interest in the township where he was building new homes, he knew all of the players in the building and zoning office which came in very handy when applying for permits and ordinances changes. Here are a few things to look for when interviewing possible attorneys for your business:

- Special knowledge in foreclosure law in the state(s) where you invest, since you will likely be buying a lot of foreclosure properties for the foreseeable future.

- A specialty in bankruptcy, since many investments come from the direct result of bankruptcies. Plus, he or she may be able to give you some solid leads on potential properties from his clients.

- Someone with plenty of referrals.

- An affordable flat fee, since paying by the hour for services can send your monthly legal fees through the roof. While uncommon if you are only planning to use an attorney once or twice, it is a deal that can be negotiated should you find yourself using his/her services more often.

If you are unable to find a qualified real estate attorney on your own, asking the people at your local bar association. They may be able to give you a list of their members.

Contractors: You will likely buy homes and apartment complexes that need some work. Having a good general contractor on retainer can save you a lot of time, energy, and money when it comes to getting the work done and finding qualified subcontractors to handle more specific jobs. If you plan on buying and holding more than just a few properties at any given time, it is usually helpful to have an in-house contractor on salary to handle any maintenance, repairs, and renovation needs that may arise, especially if you plan on renting out your investment properties while holding them for a market rebound. There is always something that needs repairing with these types of properties, and since time is money, having someone who can be called immediately can save a bundle in the long run. Just be sure that any general contractor you hire has access to a variety of other specialists, including: roofers, plumbers, electricians, tile layers, flooring specialists, siding experts, foundation professionals, and drywall specialists. Finding competent, reliable, contracting help is not as easy as it would seem. If you do not take the time to hire the right workers, you will lose valuable time and money, so be sure to use these important tips for finding both general contractors and subcontractors:

- Ask friends, neighbors, and coworkers for referrals.

- Ask the others you have worked with who they recommend. A good plumber may know a good landscaper and a great roofer may regularly work with a great electrician.

- Ask the people you meet at the local lumberyard or hardware store if they can refer someone to you.

- Check with your local zoning or code enforcement office for licensed contractors in your area.

Once you have a list of possible sources, you need to conduct a solid interview to make sure you hire the person you can trust and work with the best. The Federal Trade Commission (FTC) recommends that employers ask these questions to determine which contractor is best for you and your project:

- **How long have you been in business?** Look for well-established companies with no complaints listed with your state's consumer protection officials.

- **Are you registered and licensed with the state and local building authorities?** Only 36 states currently require contractors to be licensed to work in their state, but most municipalities require some sort of registration or licensing to work there. This may not be a guarantee of quality work, but it can help weed out unscrupulous contractors who have no intention of ever starting or finishing your project after pocketing the deposit.

- **How many projects like mine have you completed in the past year, and may I contact some of those homeowners?** Ask for a list to determine how familiar the contractor is with the type of project you want done.

- **Will you be using subcontractors?** If yes, make sure that the general contractor is liable for all payments, insurances, and licenses for them.

- **What types of insurance do you carry?** Professional contractors should have personal liability, workers' compensation, and disability and property damage coverage. Ask for copies of all insurance certificates, otherwise you may find yourself liable for any injuries or damage sustained during the renovation.

Who to Add To Your Team

When adding workers to your team, consider finding quality people in these specialty areas:

- Plumbing
- Electrical
- Roofing
- Foundations

- Tiling
- Carpet installation
- Painting
- Architectural planning
- Landscaping

An insurance agent: One of the main team members many investors overlook is a good insurance agent. You will need a lot of different types of insurance to protect your investments, so be sure to hire someone who is well versed in investment property coverage. Here is a just a sampling of some of the different types of insurance you may need to cover your assets:

- Hazard insurance: Covering fire, vandalism, theft, and other hazards on the property itself

- Flood insurance: Needed in low-lying or flood plain areas

- Specialty storm coverage: Covering damage from high winds, freezing, tornadoes, hurricanes, earthquakes, and other natural disasters and storms

- Liability insurance: Needed in the event someone is hurt on your property

- Construction insurance: Covers the property and any contractors

- Renter's insurance: Not an insurance policy you as an investor buys, but it is a good idea to urge your renter's to get it since hazard insurance only covers the property, not your renter's personal property

Marketing specialists: As you are looking for your first properties, you may not see the importance of hiring a marketing specialist for your team. Maybe you do not need one in the early stages of your new career, but you will soon enough. Marketing is an essential part of buying and selling homes in almost every region. Without the right marketing plan, your business will flounder. Be sure to look for someone who knows how to get the word out about your properties and can even find unique ways to generate a buzz about a specific property. In addition to helping you sell your investments, a good marketing specialist can also help you build your business by building your reputation as a local specialist in emerging markets and within the investment community, which can help you find more investors willing to join your team. More investors equal more money, which equals more profit.

For example, one enterprising investor decided to hold a property auction on one of their new acquisitions with a starting bid of only $3,000. Guaranteeing to sell the property for "whatever the highest bid shall be," the investor's marketing group set out to spread the word about the auction by hitting every local radio and television station the area. Several local newspapers ran stories about the sale, and hoping to generate even more interest, the marketing specialist rented parking spaces at a local shopping center and hired trolley cars to transport potential bidders to the sale a few blocks away. The buzz regarding this unique sale became so huge that the roads getting to the sale were blocked with traffic hours before the auction was scheduled to begin. In the end, 3,000 people attended the sale, with a final bid of $210,000 — more than $45,000 more than the investor had initially planned to list the property for.

Another marketing ploy this same investor used in a more depressed area was to have an essay contest for a house, giving it away to the writer of the best essay who described why they deserved a home of their own. With a $500 entrance fee and national coverage of the contest on the nation's top morning broadcast shows, the seller generated enough interest to rake in over $1 million in entrance fees for a home that was worth about $350,000 on the open market; and that he had paid about $215,000 for at a foreclosure auction. Not a bad return for taking a risk and thinking outside of the box on ways to unload a hard-to-sell property in a poor economy.

CASE STUDY: USE PANIC TO YOUR ADVANTAGE

Jason Hartman, Platinum Properties
Investment Network
www.jasonhartman.com

If one word could sum up the real estate market over the last 18 months, "panic" would be a good choice. With foreclosures in record numbers and unemployment creeping up, homeowners who have to sell their homes are definitely feeling the pressure of the uncertain market and are feeling the sting of the downturn in home prices. For seasoned investors like Jason Hartman, who has spent the last two decades building successful real estate strategies, as well as building the Platinum Properties Investment Network, Hartman Media Company, and the Jason Hartman Foundation, this panic means it is time to get in on the action.

Hartman feels that the idea of panic has helped investors feel a sense of urgency, and has driven home the idea of buying now, rather than waiting for the economy to turn around and the prices of homes go up. He is looking for prudent income properties right now, before further devaluation of the dollar occurs, and he is advising other investors to follow suit.

Interest rates are another factor in the panic of the current market. With historically low interest rates available, the time is right to buy, but loans may be harder to come by. That does not mean new investors cannot get into the market. It does, however, remind everyone that the days of easy, no-money-down financing are over. Hartman suggests some creative financing to close deals on the amazing bargains that are coming available in this panic-stricken market. One unique business model that has emerged from this financial collapse is known as the "two-step close." Essentially, companies purchase a property and make the necessary renovations, then allow an investor to refinance the property at the current market value instead of the foreclosure price. This results in a very low net down payment and allows the investor the opportunity to acquire properties for rental income that will generate the cash flow necessary to cover the expenses on the newly improved property.

This strategy that Hartman advocates makes it possible for the investor to cash in on the market and have the rental income cover expenses on the property until the market recovers and the property can be sold at a profit. His system works by capturing the increase in property value and rent that result from inflation, without falling prey to adjustable mortgage rates that would increase the overall cost of owning the property. It allows for the low payment of a more variable loan with the benefits of the fixed rate loan.

SECTION II:

Finding Hidden Bargains

Once you know what you need to look for in your investment search in emerging real estate markets, your next goal is keeping a watchful eye on the current market in order to get the most house for your dollar. This involves scoping out the best bargains and looking in places you might not think. Once you spot that perfect property with that perfect price, your investment search is not over. You will need to place an offer and secure the deal, which requires a little finessing to understand the real estate lingo and process.

Chapter 4

Bargain Hunting in Today's Market

There are a lot of bargains to be had these days for the street-wise real estate investor, but you must know when and where to look. Sure, you can head to your local real estate agent for a look at his or her listings, but the odds are you will miss a whole host of opportunities since few regular agents have access to fore-closures, liens, and other types of distressed properties. To make the most profits, you must not overlook any buying opportunity. Those who can sniff out a great deal on a distressed property generally walk away the biggest winners. So, where can you go to find the best deals?

The Local Tax Office

Investing in tax liens can yield big profits in any economy, but today's investor can see dividends of 300 percent or more if they choose the right property. What makes this type of investing even sweeter is the fact that you only need a little investment capital to get started. Some houses are sold for just a few hundred dollars, although that is unusual; the average is usually between $10,000 and $50,000. The opportunity to buy low — very low — is extremely high when investing in tax liens. As a matter of fact, many tax lien investors purchase properties for as little as a few thousand dollars and often turn around and sell them at market value, which can be anywhere from $30,000 to $200,000 — of course, most of these are in the mid-range in price and value.

Sound enticing? Around this time you may be wondering what exactly tax liens are. Basically, it is a judgment or a foreclosure on a property for an unpaid real estate or local tax bill. Every municipality charges real estate taxes to cover such services as fire, police, ambulance, roads, and schools. When these taxes go unpaid, the municipality has the legal right to put a lien on the property and sell it at an auction for the amount of taxes due. The most common are for local real estate taxes, but the state and federal government can also place a tax lien on a property. When a homeowner owes any sort of back tax liability, the governing body that is owed the tax debt can recoup that loss by placing a lien (hold) on the property. This prohibits the homeowner from selling the property until the lien is paid in full. At any time, the authority holding the lien can sell the property to recoup the price of the lien or the back taxes, including penalties and interest.

When you buy a tax lien certificate, you, the investor, are in essence giving the homeowner more time to come up with the money to pay their debt. Should they be able to come up with the money during the lien's repayment time, you will make a small sum in interest for buying the lien. Tax lien interest can range from just 2 percent to 40 percent, depending on the amount bid at the sale. In most cases, however, the homeowner is unable to pay back the lien in the time required, causing ownership of the property to be transferred to you. Essentially, you are able to purchase the property for the amount of taxes owed. This can be tens of thousands less than the value of the property — even in a depressed real estate cycle. It is common for a house worth $100,000 or more to be sold as a lien certificate for less than $25,000. Add to that the increased profit in a better real estate market, since you can command a higher selling price, and your profit margins increase even more. Keep in mind that the homeowner is not "agreeing" to this agreement; it is the law. Although the state law may allow them some extra time to come up with the money owed after the auction, they have no right to deny the tax lien sale.

Buying tax liens is a smart move for any investor since some amount of profit is always guaranteed. If the homeowner is able to buy back the lien during their redemptive period, you get interest for taking on the note. If they fail to buy back the lien, you get their property for low relative cost and can do whatever you like with it: sell it, keep it for yourself, flip it, or rent it. Buying tax liens offers little risk. Of course, you may find yourself buying a property that you cannot unload on the open market, in which case you may lose your investment. But in most cases, tax liens offer only profit potential. There are some things to watch out for to guarantee the most profit, though.

- **Check out the property first:** Most tax liens are sold as-is from the courthouse. Little, if any, information is offered about the property beyond its address and the amount of the lien, making it vitally important to get a list of the addresses of properties for sale before the auction and to check out the properties you are interested in on your own. Keep in mind that no walkthroughs or inspections are allowed. Still, you should at least look at a property if you are thinking of buying its tax lien.

- **Understand the rules of local tax lien sales:** Every state and municipality has its own rules regarding taking possession of a tax lien. Some offer redemptive periods, in which the owner can pay you back and get their property back; others offer total auction sales where you take immediate ownership. Be sure you know what they are before investing in any lien certificate.

- **Have cash ready:** The one drawback to tax lien investing is the need for cash. These sales require at least 10 percent down at the time of purchase with a final cash payment within one to three days. Financing is rarely available for this type of property purchase, so you will have to have the money necessary to make the sale. So, if you can buy a tax lien on a $100,000 house for $25,000, you will need to have the entire $25,000 available in cash the day of the sale.

Types of Tax Liens Available

- Local real estate liens: Liens placed on a property for unpaid local or state property taxes.

- Federal liens: Liens placed on a property to satisfy an unpaid income tax debt.

- Mechanic's liens: Liens placed on a property owner by a building contractor, plumber, electrician, or landscaper for nonpayment of services.

- Mortgages: The most common lien. In the event that a mortgage goes unpaid, the lender can place a lien on the property and force its sale to recoup their lost investment.

- Attorney's liens: Attorneys offer a service for a fee. When that fee goes unpaid, they have the legal right to place a retaining lien on the client's personal or real estate property to recoup their lost revenue.

Where to find tax liens

Finding tax liens takes a bit of sleuthing. Even though tax lien information is public record and access cannot be denied, it is not always easy to get your hands on. Not every tax office is good at keeping records and the people at the front desk may not know off-hand where you can find the information you need. Some may not even have the office personnel to help you and may even require you to do your own digging to uncover a list of liens.

To find a listing of local and county tax liens coming up for auction, visit the local tax office and ask to see its records. Some are very organized and have listings already available for prospective buyers, but many smaller municipalities are not. State lien records are also usually housed in the state tax office at the state capitol and are easier to access. The CCH *Standard Federal*

Tax Reporter® (**www.tax.cchgroup.com/FED**) is an excellent source for finding tax liens in a specific geographic area. It is produced by the federal government, and lists tax lien properties by area. The tax reporter can be purchased in either CD, print form from its Web site (**www.onlinestore.cch.com**), or can be reviewed for free at many large-scale public libraries or university libraries.

When searching any database for tax lien records, there are many different search options available, including:

- State
- County
- Municipality
- Address
- Owner's name
- Type of property
- Amount of taxes owed
- Date of lien sale

How tax lien sales work

Once a tax lien has been filed on a property, the governing authority has the legal right to sell it outright in a deed sale (also called an over-the-counter sale), or offer the lien for sale in a tax lien certificate auction, which is the most common form of lien sales.

Any type of tax lien sale can be held monthly, quarterly, or annually, depending on the number of liens a municipality has on file. Bigger cities hold them more often than smaller, more rural ones do. The dates of sales are usually posted in the tax office and may be found in the classified section of the local newspaper. These sales are usually held in the county court-house. Buyers must be registered with the auctioneer in order to bid, and proof of payment must be shown. This can be in the form of a certified check or a letter from your bank. Most tax lien sales are held a bit differently than auctions. It does not matter whether it is a deed sale or a lien sale: The auction process is the same. Before wielding your paddle to attempt winning a tax lien, be aware of some of the basics of bidding:

Bidding down the interest: In the process of bidding down interest, bidders can decide the amount of the interest they will agree to before buying a tax lien certificate. This method is important in the event that, after the sale, the homeowner decides to repurchase the lien.

Bidding down the ownership: In Iowa, investors can some-times bid down the ownership at some tax lien auctions. That means that the buyer can actually only pay a portion of the auction price for only part ownership in the property. For instance, if they bid ownership down to 50 percent, they will only own half of the property, and thus only be entitled to half of the profits when it is sold. The state of Iowa takes the rest of the cut.

Random selection: This type of auction draws specific bidder numbers at random, either by hand or by computer genera-tion, for each tax lien being sold at the auction. If your number is pulled, you win the auction for the amount of taxes due.

Premium bidding: This is much more like a traditional auc-tion where the highest bidder takes all, even if that means pay-ing more than just the outstanding tax bill.

Off-the-shelf buying: In some areas, tax liens can be bought straight from the tax collector for the amount of taxes owed. These are often properties that have already been up for auction and have not been purchased for one reason or another.

Participating in the tax lien bidding process is not difficult; you just need to take time to learn the ropes and figure out how it is handled in the area where you are interested in obtaining properties.

REO Properties: Real Estate or Bank Owned

Real estate owned (REO) properties grew in interest around 2007 and continued to remain popular mainly because investors understood them more. Part of the reason is because there is such a large inventory of them available. When a bank or other lender forecloses on a house, it becomes real estate owned, otherwise known as bank owned. Once the bank takes formal possession of the property, it is free to sell it to anyone via its own selling agent. While many REO properties are eventually put up for auction, the best time to buy is usually in the early stages of its acquisition because you can get them cheaper. Once a bank puts a property up for auction, the bank has invested more money into the property for such things as auction and Realtor fees. This means the bank must get more money out of the property. Some of the benefits of buying REO properties directly from the bank include:

- **The ability to inspect the property:** Oftentimes, pre-fore-closures or auction sales prohibit any type of inspection of a property. Some do not even a allow walkthroughs prior to the sale. REO properties almost always allow potential buyers to preview and inspect the property before buying it. This can be a big plus when it comes to understanding what you are buying and not paying too much.

- **The ability to negotiate a lower price:** Like any other type of real estate for sale, the price of a post-foreclosure REO can be negotiated.

- **The sellers are motivated to sell:** In the midst of the greatest foreclosure crisis since the great depression, banks are being left with thousands of properties to pay taxes on and keep maintained. This leaves them very eager to sell off some of their foreclosure inventory, which can mean great buys for investors.

- **Due diligence applies:** This can give an investor time to have a property checked out more thoroughly once an offer has been made. Should problems be uncovered, the buyer has the legal right to back out of the deal without penalty.

- **All REO property titles are clear:** When you buy a property at an auction, there is no guarantee that the title has been cleared and that no other liens are being held on the property. That could mean that the new owner owes money on the property he or she did not know about or anticipate. But, when you buy a REO property, you are guaranteed that the title has been cleared and there are no other debts open on the house or land.

- **Financing is available:** When buying a pre-foreclosure or a property at an auction, you must have cash in hand. This is not the case with REO properties. Many lenders actually offer their own financing to qualified investment buyers. This can make the transaction much easier for all involved.

Here are some of the disadvantages of buying a REO property. First, most sales are considered as-is, which means if you do not notice a problem with a property until after the sale is finalized, there is nothing you can do to make the seller (the bank) pay for repair costs. Second, there may be extra paper-work involved in the buying process, since the bank owns the property. Finally, the bank is usually unable to supply normal disclosures regarding the property, since they have no idea what has been done to it or what problems may have been an issue with it in recent years. This can result in unknown problems to deal with.

Buying Bulk Can Save You Even More

While banks are usually more than willing to sell just one or two REO properties to an interested buyer, those willing to take package deals can negotiate an even better price. Banks want (and need) to get as many of their foreclosures off their books as soon as possible, so if an investor comes forward who is willing to buy 10, 20, or 100 properties from the bank's inventory, they can usually strike an impressive deal.

Be warned: Buying in bulk can be a dangerous endeavor for the inexperienced REO investor. Almost every bulk package includes some fixer-upper properties or those that are not worth much — if anything — on the open market. Even if you have to donate these properties to a local town for a park or a local church for a parking lot, you will likely make enough profit on the other houses you obtain in the package to make it worth your investment. The key to making the bulk buy is getting the entire package for such a small amount that the sale of just one or two of the homes covers the initial investment in full, leaving the rest of those sales as pure profit.

Mortgage assumption

There are situations in which an investor can assume, or take over, a homeowner's mortgage without paying anything else for the house. Not every mortgage qualifies for an assumption, but if it does, it can be a great way for a strapped homeowner to get out from underneath a burdening mortgage debt. It can also be a good way for an investor to get a certain property for less than an open-market sale — plus, the investor can save thousands in closing costs.

As the name applies, a mortgage assumption means that the owner of a property signs over the deed, along with the debt attached to the property (the mortgage and any equity credit that has been taken against it). The investor is then responsible for paying off the mortgage, either in one lump sum or through the monthly payments the first homeowner was making. The homeowner may not accept any additional payments for the property. In many cases, this scenario does not work well for investors, since there may not be enough equity in the home to make sense buying it in this manner. If, however, a homeowner must get out from underneath their mortgage despite the equity they may have in the house, it can be a good investment. This is usually only the case when a homeowner is so desperate to save his or her credit rating and FICO score that they gladly give up any equity they have built in their home to get out from underneath their mortgage obligation. The key to making a mortgage assumption work for an investor is to get the home for a low enough payment and final payoff so as to make the same profit as he or she would get buying another property through another buying opportunity.

Property auctions

There are several different types of property auctions that can yield a good buy in addition to the tax lien auction. Sometimes, a property owner will try to make a quick sale by auctioning off their property, but this rarely yields a good enough buy for the emerging markets investor. The best auction scenario for the investor is the foreclosure auction. There are plenty of advantages to buying a foreclosure property at an auction, but the biggest is a low starting bid. Most property auctions begin with a bid as low as the amount owed on the mortgage. While prices can go up from there, many are sold for that amount, which can be as much as 75 percent less than the property's appraised value. As is the case with most investment opportunities, buying property at an auction comes with its own set of disadvantages.

- **Little, if any, information offered on the property:** Most foreclosure auctions take place in the courthouse with only the address given to prospective buyers, which can make the process of buying properties harrowing. Prior investigation might not have been done to learn everything about a specific property before bidding.

- **Immediate payment:** Most auctions require a 10 percent down payment, with the balance due within 24 hours.

- **The title is not always clear on these properties:** This is especially true if you are purchasing a junior lien.

- **The possibility of reinstatement to the previous owners:** In some states, the owners can get their house back even after it has been auctioned off, as long as they pay off the mortgage, plus penalties and interest, within a specified time period. This can be anywhere from three months to two years.

- **The need to evict current residents:** Many foreclosure auction homes remain lived in, making it necessary to evict all current occupants. This can be a real time-consuming hassle, which can leave an investor frustrated.

Leasing options

Leasing options can be a good way to test the waters regarding the rental and purchase of a property without shelling out thousands of dollars to actually buy it. How does it work? First, find a seller who is also agreeable to renting out their property. This is usually quite easy in a down market where sales are slim. This allows the owner to keep up with his or her mortgage and taxes without straining his or her own personal finances.

Next, you enter into a lease agreement, which gives you control over the property for a specified period of time without actually owning it. For instance, you may lease the property for a period of two years for $900 with the option to purchase the property at the end of the lease for $75,000.

Once you have control of the property through the lease, you can rent it to anyone else for any amount of money. This gives you time to find suitable renters, wait for the market to rebound, and get your investment income together.

At the end of the lease, you can either walk away without owing the property owner anything else or you can buy the property for the agreed amount. Should the value of the property slide even further, you can walk away without losing your investment. If the value rises, you still get to buy it for the lower amount, as stated in the option agreement.

Lease options can be a great way for a new investor to see what the market will do over a certain period of time, decide if the property in question is a good deal, find long-term renters, and decide if he or she really wants the property in his or her inventory after all.

New Construction

It may sound crazy to buy a developer's leftovers when new construction has come to a halt. Buying new construction when no one is buying certainly holds a lot of risk, but consider the payoff if you make wise choices. Why would a builder be willing to sell off some of his or her inventory (finished home, partially finished, or land tracts) far below its value, especially when the builder knows as well as you that the market will rebound and profits will abound? Simple: Developers are not in the business of renting, leasing, or otherwise holding property. They want a clean, fast, in-and-out deal. They want to buy a good tract of land; build the appropriate housing, offices, or retail shops in it; and sell, get out, and move onto their next big project.

A development that stands partially finished or partially sold is a big headache for developers. They must continue to maintain the roads and utilities for unfinished projects. In most cases, they also have hundreds of thousands of dollars held in escrow by the municipality where the development is located as a sort of bank account against problems which may occur, such as a stalled development. The longer it takes to finish the project, the longer the escrow money is held. However, if developers sell the property, their escrow money is returned and the new owner is responsible for re-establishing the escrow account.

Many municipalities require builders to place a certain percentage of the total cost of a project in an escrow account to pay for roads, improvements, sidewalks, sewer lines, and landscaping if the developer should ever bail. This money cannot be refunded until the project is satisfactorily completed or sold to a new owner. By selling the end units of a project or partially finished homes within a development, the builder can walk away with the escrow money back in his or her pocket. The loss of a few thousands dollars is worth a quick exit to many builders unwilling to wait for the market to turn around in lieu of a bigger payday.

Of course, finding these types of properties requires having some eyes and ears in the building business. You must have contacts with a developer, a township or county office, or even with a popular lender to alert you of prospects. This is not usually an avenue that a brand new investor can use, since he or she has not had time to build a good professional network. Once you get to know the players in your area, however, it can be a useful strategy for making money.

So, what are the benefits of buying new construction?

- You have "new" properties to sell, which are generally more desirable than older ones.

- Even unfinished buildings hold a lot of profit potential once finished.

- Most land contracts already have built-in construction approvals from the local zoning and building offices.

- If you are lucky enough to land a finished property sale, you will have the added benefit of having high-end upgrades that make a home easier to sell for a higher price.

- Most new construction is positioned in great neighborhoods, making it easier to sell.

- Oftentimes, an investor can convince a builder to finance the buy, making an outside mortgage unnecessary and saving time, trouble, and finance charges.

Coupled with these benefits are the drawbacks. New construction can be risky because:

- There is a chance the market in that area will never rebound sufficiently to finish and profit from a large-scale project.

- Buying a property in an unfinished neighborhood can be next-to-impossible to sell if buyers are fearful that the neighborhood will not be finished in a reasonable amount of time. In this case, you better make sure you can guarantee potential buyers that construction is continuing and the project definitely has an end date.

- Unfinished houses may need to be demolished if not completed or sold in the right amount of time, which can cost an investor more cash than expected.

- Unless you investigate the entire project, you may inherit more problems than you anticipate in regards to zoning and building permissions, approvals, and restrictions. The key to avoiding these issues is to make sure the developer selling the property already has approvals and variances.

- Some builders simply overdevelop areas and may be trying to unload an unsalable property.

Other Places to Find Good Deals

Most people know the above-mentioned places offer good bargains in real estate. However, consider using one of these lesser-known avenues to find and buy your next investment property.

Law Enforcement Seizures

One way to get your hands on cheap properties is to look for seizures under the Racketeer Influenced and Corrupt Organizations Act (RICO), a federal law that allows local, state and federal law enforcement agencies to seize the personal property and real estate of arrested criminals. Finding local listings of these properties can be done one of two ways:

1. Checking for a listing at your local sheriff's office

2. Checking the U.S. Marshals Service Web site (**www.justice.gov/marshals**)

Probate

People who inherit a property often want a quick sale to unload the burden of caring for a house they have no intention of living in. One way to locate these great finds is to work with a probate attorney in the area you are interested in investing in. Let the attorney know that you are in the market for any properties that might go up for sale through his or her office or clients.

Vacant Properties

Drive around any small town or big city and you will eventually come across a few vacant buildings or lots. Although these properties are typically in need of repair, they can often be purchased for next-to-nothing. To find the owner of the house or lot, simply go to the local tax office with the address. Once you find the owner, send him or her a handwritten note that tells them you are interested in buying the property.

HUD and VA Auctions

The IRS or local tax office are not the only ones who auction off real estate. The Department of Housing and Urban Development also periodically auctions off foreclosed properties on which they hold a mortgage. The U.S. Department of Veterans Affairs, too, forecloses on defaulted loans and often sells these foreclosures at an auction when they cannot sell them though a Realtor.

Why the IRS is your friend

When you think of the IRS, you may consider them "the enemy." Well, not anymore. The IRS can be a friend of the real estate investors, offering a myriad of tax breaks and loopholes that can be used to make even more money. Of course, the tax code changes periodically (sometimes even from year to year), so instead of discussing specific programs and codes, this section will concentrate on the generic rules that apply to investment properties. Want to learn more? Here are some of the most common tax breaks the government offers to investors right now:

Expenses

The key to keeping your taxes down when investing is to keep your expenses high, at least on paper. This does not mean you should lie on your tax return; instead, sue every allowable expense the government offers to bring down both your investment income and your personal income.

Most basic costs of running a business are deductible (the for-rent ad running in the local paper or repair costs, for example), but you can also deduct a certain portion of the cost of your investment property each year as depreciation. A residential property can be depreciated over the course of 27 ½ years and a commercial property over 39 years. That means that if you paid $100,000 for a rental property, you can depreciate 1/27th of the cost each year for 27 years. That, along with your other deductions, can help reduce your overall taxable income. Keep in mind that this tax break is for small investors only. Those with an adjusted income of $150,000 or more do not qualify for this added depreciation deduction.

The 1031 Exchange

Annual deductions for many investors do not cover their overall tax bill, but there are other ways to get back some of that tax money when you finally sell the investment property. The best way to avoid paying taxes from a sale is to buy another property of equal or greater value. The IRS calls this a 1031 exchange. Emerging markets specialists especially like this tax loophole because it can keep them from paying taxes on the income generated through the sale of their properties for an indefinite period of time.

It works like this: You buy a property for $40,000 and fix it up. As you are fixing it up you scout out another investment property you want to buy. As soon as you have a buyer for the improved property (at a profit of course), you set the deal for the new purchase using the profits from your sale. If you can close the deal within 45 days of the first sale, you do not have to pay taxes on the profits generated form the first property's sale.

This is an excellent way to continue to upgrade your investments without paying the IRS the 35 percent tax bill you might otherwise owe. This strategy also works well if you use the profits from one investment to buy a rental property, since the taxes for any sale will not come due until you ultimately sell the second property. Even still, you will only owe the taxes for the property sold, not the original ones under the 1031 loophole.

Capital Gains

There are two important taxes to be aware of when investing in real estate: the short and long term capital gains taxes. Many flippers in recent years were not aware of the difference and ended up losing big to the IRS at tax time.

Capital gains are extra taxes due on investment income. If you invest in a short-term property (holding it for less than one year) you could end up paying a substantial amount (35–40 percent) on the profits generated in short-term capital gains taxes. Hold onto that property for 13 months or more and that tax liability shrinks to just 15 percent using the long-term capital gains rules. Since emerging markets are usually a long-term investment, the capital gains discrepancy usually works in the investor's favor. However, it is important to watch the calendar carefully when dealing with short-term investments. After all, who wants to sell a property in the 11th month and pay an extra 15–20 percent in taxes when they may be able to hold off settlement and bank that extra money?

Accumulated Losses

For larger-scale investors, accumulated losses from all of your holdings can be used when you sell one property to avoid a big tax bill. All you have to do is keep track of those losses over a period of years, carrying them over from one tax year to the next until you need them. This is a good strategy for an investor who foresees a big payday down the line.

The Primary Residence Loophole

If you are an emerging markets investor who has been lucky enough to get your hands on a deep-discounted high-yield property, you will want to make plans for the day you sell it for three or four times what you paid. High-end properties that sell for hundreds of thousands of dollars can come with a hefty tax bill when sold — unless you plan ahead. A good strategy in this market is to turn that investment property into your primary residence. That does not mean you can rent out a portion of it or that you have to live there year-round, but it does have to be the primary residence listed on your driver's license, tax records, work records, and other official forms. If you live in the property for two of the next five years before it is sold, you can get out of paying much in profit taxes on the sale. This can be great news for smaller investors who get their hands on a big profit-maker that they plan to hold for a while.

Social Security and Medicare Loophole

Real estate investors are exempt from paying social security and Medicare on their investment income. Rental income is not considered "earned income" and is therefore exempt from most self-employment taxes. However, this means that you will not qualify for these benefits in the future if real estate investing is your main, or only, source of income.

As you can see, there are quite a few ways to limit your tax liability when investing in emerging markets. Of course, a qualified tax professional can tell you about dozens of other loopholes that you may qualify for. The point is to be honest with the IRS and reasonable with your deductions. If you follow those basic rules, the odds are that the IRS will never question what you state on your tax return.

CASE STUDY: THE UNDER-WEAR OF REAL ESTATE

George Moskoff,
management consultant
www.thehousefixupguy.com

Ask George Moskoff about flipping houses, and he will be sure to correct you — what he does is much more than the type of quick cosmetic fixes you see on home improvement shows. Moskoff, a successful management consultant and licensed contractor, knows what he is talking about from having purchased and sold more than 14 investment properties. The last property he sold was at the height of the market. He still owns one property that he is keeping as a rental, waiting out the drop in housing prices that has hit his home state of California, as well as neighboring Arizona and Nevada, harder than many other areas in the country.

As for his take on investment properties, he goes for quality improvements, what he calls the "underwear" of the house. What we all see on TV is granite countertops and new paint, but Moskoff emphasizes focusing first on the basic necessities. Is the roof leaking? Is the furnace broken? Is there a furnace at all? Before even considering aesthetic changes, a property needs to meet the standard of safety and completion.

The next thing Moskoff considers with the resale of a home is how the prospective buyer (usually the woman) views the home. The way we live has changed drastically over the last several decades, and if you are considering an investment property that was built even 20 years ago, it does not have that instant appeal to new buyers. Buyers like open spaces with large kitchens that overlook family or living rooms. Great rooms are common in new construction and can be created when you take the time to do the quality, well-planned renovation that Moskoff does.

He always looks through the eyes of the buyer, although he admits to having personal preferences, such as glass front doors and large windows. He looks for ways to open up smaller rooms, taking out walls and headers to make way for the larger kitchens and shared spaces that modern families look for in their homes.

With so much upheaval in the real estate market, many people wonder if there is any money to be made at all. Moskoff would advise new investors to approach investment properties as a longer-term investment than they would have been in the past when a quick turnaround was the norm. Buying a foreclosure or low-price property with the intention to hold onto it until the market appreciates is the best way to make money in this climate. Holding off on improvements until the market picks up, all while renting the property, is another great way to make the market work in your favor.

Chapter 5

Closing the Deal

Anyone who has ever tried to strike a deal knows the art and skill involved in negotiating a winning purchase agreement aimed at generating real profits. There is more to finding great profit-potential properties than there is to buying a cheap house. You must know which house is poised to bring in the highest return, and then negotiate the best price you can. This can only be done by learning how to predict the next emerging market, finding the perfect house, driving the best bargain, and sealing the deal. If you are new at the emerging markets game, you will want to learn about these important topics before making an offer on your first investment property.

Know Exactly What You Are Bidding On

You think you have found the perfect investment property — it seems to be in a good neighborhood that shows signs of turning around anytime soon. The price is at least 25 percent below market value, the property seems to fit several demographic buyers groups, and the sellers are eager to strike a deal. Before you pull out your checkbook, take a closer look. Oftentimes, what appears to be a real gem in the investment world is really a sinkhole waiting to eat away at your bank account — and your nerves. When looking at a house to buy, check out these basic problem areas to determine if this property is worth a more detailed second glance.

1. Structure: If there is one thing you will want when buying an investment property, it is a solid structure. Look for uneven or bowing floors, corners, and walls. Sure, settling can cause a wall to be off plumb, but a floor that does not feel solid could be a problem.

2. Water Control: Do you notice any signs of water damage? Does the basement floor feel damp or look as if it has been flooded in the past? Also, check the slope of the property to ensure that water is being drained away from the foundation, not towards it.

3. Roof: The cost of a new roof can be expensive, so make sure the roof on the building you are considering is at least in decent shape. Otherwise, you should factor in extra cost when determining what you can pay for the property.

4. Details: A house featuring unique moldings, tile work, hardware, and other finishing touches will not only be easier to sell, but it will command a higher price. Watch out for these types of selling points when taking your first look at a property.

5. Plumbing: Most investors know enough to check for plumbing leaks when looking over a house, but also remember to check the water pressure. Can you run the shower and the dishwasher at the same time? Do all the sinks and toilets work properly, or will they need repairs? These are all costs you must consider when determining a buying price.

6. Electrical System: One basic to look for is whether or not there are a sufficient number of electrical receptacles in each room to meet both a buyer's needs and local ordinances. When considering an older home, make sure it offers at least 100 amp service, or you may find a major upgrade necessary to obtain hazard insurance.

7. Heating System: Some questions to ask in regards to the heating system include:

- What type of heat does the house use?
- Does it offer central air?
- Are there enough registers for the size of the house?
- Is zoned heat/air needed for comfort? If so, does the house offer it?
- Are all the rooms heated?

8. Energy Efficiency: Today's buyers are looking for energy efficiency, and that means having the right type and amount of insulation — at least R-19 in moderate climates and up to R-38 for colder climates. To check for wall insulation, simply remove a receptacle cover on a perimeter wall. Windows and doors must also be in good working order, and be thick enough to keep out the cold. Older windows will likely have to be replaced to sell for a higher price later on, which can get pricey.

9. Fireplaces: A fireplace can add a lot of value to a home, but only if it is in working order. Make sure to have the chimney and fireplace checked to ensure you will not have any high repair costs later.

10. The Aesthetics: Curb appeal is essential to making a sale, so make sure you are prepared to make your investment property look its best form the outside. This includes a fresh coat of paint, new siding, landscaping, etc. The more work left undone now is more work and expenses for you when it comes time to sell.

Hiring a Professional Home Inspector

Most investors possess enough knowledge to see basic problems with a property, but they rarely have the experience to find more serious problems that may be lurking inside the walls of a home. It is always best to bring in a qualified property inspector to do a thorough check on a possible investment.

A proficient examiner has the knowledge and experience to check both the interior and exterior of a property to find defects and problems. Oftentimes, they can tell you about problems the house encountered and fixed in the past, and can even give you a detailed list of future maintenance projects. An inspector's report is not just important to understanding what is needed to get a specific property up to par: It is essential to your bottom line. Without a realistic understanding of a home's flaws, you will have no idea how much to bid on the house. When hiring a home inspector to review the possibilities of your property, double-check that he or she has the experience to find the kinds of problems you want to avoid. There are currently three national organizations that offer education and certificate programs for home inspectors:

1. **American Society of Home Inspectors (www.ashi. org):** The oldest (and largest) professional organization for home inspectors in the United States. This nonprofit sets the standards and code of ethics for home inspections, as well as information for real estate professionals and consumers.

2. **National Association of Home Inspectors (www.nahi. org):** Promotes and certifies national home inspector, as well as educates and informs the public about professional home inspections.

3. **International Association of Certified Home Inspectors (www.nachi.org):** A worldwide nonprofit inspection association.

Although you are not guaranteed a perfect inspector by hiring someone holding one of these organizations' certifications, you can feel more at ease knowing that the inspector you chose has at least been educated in the field. Other things to look for in a home inspector include: proper licensing, insurance, on-the-job experiences (a retired contractor, electrician or plumber often makes an excellent inspector), and references. Do not be afraid to ask a potential inspector how many inspections they do every year — the more the better. Experience counts for a lot in this business.

Here are a few other questions to ask when choosing an inspector.

- **Will I receive an immediate report, or will I have to wait for a written report?** This may or may not matter to you, but it is important information to have on-hand.

- **Is the final inspection report detailed, or does it just offer a checklist format?** Checklist reports often miss the exact type of information you need to make a decision regarding a property acquisition.

- **Do you check for radon, termite, and well and septic problems?** Not every inspector does, so make sure you know what services you are buying. Just because an inspector does not feel qualified to check for termites or well issues does not make them a bad inspector, but it does mean you will have to hire another person to come out and check those areas.

- **Do you regularly attend training seminars and conferences to keep up with new trends, regulations and the like?**

- **What is the cost of the inspection?** Home inspection fees range from a minimal $100 to thousands of dollars, depending on the type of inspection being done, how much information the buyer is after, and how much experience the inspector has.

Once the inspection is complete, you will have to review the report and factor in the cost of all necessary repairs, suggested renovations, maintenance, and other upgrades. Include the cost of everything on your inspector's list, plus the items you personally want to upgrade in an attempt to garner a higher selling price later. Consider how much you plan to sell the property for and see if your profit margin is big enough. If not, you may want to consider offering a lower bid than the asking price.

Did You Know:

You do not have to wait until all of your inspections are done before putting in a bid for the property, thus possibly losing it to another investor. Make the best bid you can with the minimal knowledge you have, and use the 30–90 day due-diligence period to get your inspections, review your costs, and determine if a bid change is necessary.

Driving a Hard Bargain

When it comes to getting the absolute best price on a property, it is crucial to become a master negotiator. Until you can learn how to negotiate the best deal, odds are you will pay too much.

What is negotiation?

Getting each property for the amount you want requires negotiating with its seller. Sometimes it is easy to drive down the price of a property, and sometimes it is not.

Negotiation is simple two parties settling on a mutually beneficial solution to an issue, The problem is, most people think of the negotiation process as a fight against each other. If you pit yourself against the seller, someone is going to lose — and that someone could be you. A better tactic is to come to the negotiation table with a positive attitude. Try to find a price you can both agree on so neither you nor the seller feel taken advantage of. Sometimes that means paying a few thousand more for a property, but consider the benefit a fair negotiation offers down the road. If this seller believes you struck a good deal, he or she will be more willing to sell you other properties in the future. Even if this is a one-time property sale, the positive word-of-mouth the seller gives you is good for business.

To become a master negotiator, remember these basic tips:

1. Consider price negotiations as a discussion, not a confrontation. Negotiating means that each party gives up a little bit until an amicable price is reached. Come to

the table understanding that you are not going to walk away with a house for 10 percent of its value; by the same token, the seller understands that an investment property will not be sold for its full value.

2. Never show your emotions. Stay calm and collected even if you get angry or feel like you are being taken advantage of. Remember, there are other properties to buy, so move on if you cannot compromise.

3. Consider the seller — there may be more at stake here than you are aware. Maybe there is an emotional attachment to this house, or perhaps the seller needs a certain amount of money for a specific purpose. Not everyone is out to rake you over the coals, so be sensitive to the seller's needs. That does not mean, however, that you have to meet their price demands.

Never negotiate like you are out for blood. Be assertive, yet fair; otherwise, you will get a reputation for "stealing" properties, which is never good for business. A well-done negotiation leaves both parties feeling satisfied, as if they got the best deal they could at the time. Be willing to give and take to get what you really want — your next investment property.

Buyer beware: Haggling is less of an option

In 2009, haggling for a lower sales price was not just a good idea, it was expected. That trend is changing, however, and buyers need to be aware of it. Today's sellers realize that the high prices of five or six years ago are gone, yet they still do not want to settle for less than they should, so many are beginning to heed their real estate agent's advice and price their properties more realistically, according to statistics gathered from the Altos Research, which watches real estate sales trends.

According to Altos Research, only about 1/3 of home sellers will now lower their asking price when interest is shown on a property. What does that mean for emerging market specialists? Look for properties that have an asking price you can deal with because trying to push a seller into selling it to you lower may backfire, causing you to lose the deal altogether. What is causing this sudden unwillingness by sellers to negotiate a lower price? There are several factors influencing these decisions, according to the experts at the National Association of Realtors:

- Most Realtors are urging their clients to price their homes right from the beginning. Asking too high of a price forces reductions later, which could signal panic to a prospective buyer, thus causing the price to drop even further.

- Although it is by no means a seller's market (it probably will not become one for several more years), the market is loosening up a bit in many areas, creating more competition.

- It is not taking as much time to sell a home these days, which tends to make sellers a bit more confident.

- Foreclosures are on a downward trend, which helps stabilize housing prices.

Does this mean that emerging market buyers will not be able to find good deals? Of course not. What it does mean is that as an investor, you will not have to worry as much about the negotiation process as you once did and will have to seek out properties with a sales price you are comfortable with.

Divvying out the costs

Striking the best deal possible on any investment property requires more than an understanding of your purchase and maintenance costs — it requires having a solid understanding of all costs associated with the property. If you fail to account for these costs, you can quickly see your profit margin shrink. Be sure to obtain a complete listing of purchase costs, including, but not limited to:

- Local taxes
- Title fees
- County fees
- Use and occupancy permit fees
- Escrow monies needed for utilities, garbage, or sewer
- Buyer's premium

If you are using a real estate agent, he or she will be able to provide you with a complete list of closing costs. If not, it is your job to find out what fees apply in your area and how much they total.

Sometimes it is simply not possible to get the seller to agree to a lower price on the property. That does not mean, however, that you can drive a hard bargain. Take a look at all of the renovation and maintenance items on your list, as well as the closing costs associated with buying the house. Can you get the seller to agree to take on some of this expense or work? Oftentimes, a seller will agree to make general fixes to a property or even pick up some or all of the closing costs to get their asking price.

In some instances, you may even get a seller to agree to a major renovation or improvement to the house in order to make the sale. This is great for you bottom line, so go for it. Every little bit you can get a seller to do for you is less work and money you have to put in once the house is yours.

Sealing the Deal

Once you and the seller have come to an agreement on the price of the property, it is time to seal the deal. This requires a little extra work and some care regarding the details of the sale. Make a wrong move here and you could end up paying too much for the property.

One of the most important things you can do to ensure an equitable deal is to have your legal department (real estate attorney) look over the paperwork. Be sure that there are no unexpected clauses or contingencies in it that you may regret later. Also, be sure that each party understands what they are responsible for in regards to the final sale. For instance, if you want the seller to clean out the overstuffed garage of garbage, be sure that is in your contract. Otherwise, you may end up spending hundreds of dollars for someone to come do it for you. If there are repairs you would like handled prior to closing, clearly list them in the sales agreement. Likewise, if the seller only wants an as-is sale, then you must take responsibility for all clean up and repairs of the property on your own. The best thing you can do to ensure a hassle-free sale is to keep the lines of communication open with the seller and put every request in writing, no matter how small or insignificant it may seem.

Tips for a Winning Agreement

1. Ask important questions. Find out from the seller exactly what needs to be done to make the sale happen.

2. State your needs. Sometimes you can negotiate other things instead of a price reduction. For instance, maybe the seller cannot lower the price of the property, but he or she can fix the roof or do some landscaping to help you save money in the long run.

3. Offer some options. Instead of stubbornly having only one offer, consider other options, such as having the seller pay the closing costs on the deal.

4. Avoid an argument. When you argue, you make the other person feel as if they must prove you wrong. That is detrimental to a negotiation. Be assertive but in a more gentile way.

Read the sales agreement carefully

Whether you use an attorney or real estate professional to handle your transaction, make sure you carefully read over the sales agreement to ensure that you are getting exactly what you want. Most new investors tend to make a critical mistake when reviewing their first few sales agreements. They verify the main points, like the sales price, closing date, and terms of payment, but fail to thoroughly go over the more minute details. Unfortunately, not covering these smaller details before the sale could spell out big trouble for you after the sale.

For instance, all disclosures regarding the property should be clearly outlined in the sales agreement. Say that the seller promises you the house has never experienced a water problem, but you find out a year later that it had been flooded previously. Many states let you consult the seller for the cost of fixing any problems related to water damage, but only if you have a clear disclosure statement in the sales agreement. Of course, if you are buying a house as-is, which is usually the case in regards to foreclosure and bank-owned properties, disclosures are not included in the sale. Instead, you are purchasing both the property and its problems without question.

What are some of the things that should be drafted in your sales agreement? Here are a few of the basics.

- An outline of the title you will be receiving. This will tell you the exact perimeters of the building and lot for which you are buying, plus ownership legalities.

- The clearly stated due diligence time period. This is the time you have to make your inspections and either renegotiate the sales price or pull out of the deal completely.

- All agreements associated with handling any deposit monies: Will it be put into escrow? Under what circumstances can it be refunded?

Title companies, escrow, and closing

Hiring a good title company is extremely important, especially if you will be investing in distressed or foreclosed properties. A clear title, otherwise known as a property with no liens on it, is essential to safeguard your investment. Should you purchase a property with liens, you as the new owner will be responsible for paying them off. When you hire a title company to conduct a thorough title search, you are also buying an insurance policy that verifies their findings. Should they miss something in the back history of the property, the insurance will pay you any legal fees and other judgments to have the title cleared at a later date.

In addition to searching a property's history, your title company will also hold all escrow monies for you and the seller, and handle the details of the closing. This includes paying off old lenders at closing and enacting any new mortgage on the property. If there is a profit to be made, the seller will receive it at the closing table as soon as all legal documents are signed. In some states, both the buyer and seller, along with their representatives, are required to appear at the closing table. In other states, it can all be handled via mail or fax. Make certain you understand the rules of closing in your area or state when setting the date for the final transfer to take place. Closing is an important day in the life of a real estate investor. It is the day you take possession of a brand new investment property.

SECTION III:

Financing Your Investments

Once you have found your ideal market for investing and hunted out the best purchase prices possible, your next goal is to get your finances in order so you can cover your offer and your investment — and still have enough for day-to-day life. This could involve taking hard look at your expenses, determining if you should apply for a loan (and determine which type of loan) to cover some costs, or looking to other investors to buy in to your investment.

Chapter 6

What Are You Willing to Pay?

If there is one thing you must always keep in mind when looking for new emerging market, it is the price you are willing to pay. If you lose sight of or have not set your financial limits, you will not make it in the emerging markets business long. The absolute worst thing a real estate investor can do is get in over his or her head financially. Avoid this situation by knowing what you can afford when evaluating each new prospect.

But, how can you clearly establish a budget for new acquisitions and figure out the capital you need to maintain the investments you already have?

What You Need to Live On vs. What You Have to Invest

When it comes to making money in real estate, balance is key. When it comes to your finances, you will end up stressed, overworked, and miserable without the right balance. Keep your end result in focus and take each step with caution, and you will make money. Getting rich in emerging markets takes time, and if you are in too much of a hurry, you will lose more than your bank account.

The first aspects you must establish in your financial life are your living expenses versus your investment expenses. Both are important and should not be overlooked when determining an investment budget. Your living expenses — the money you need to pay your personal bills each month — must be met either though a primary job or your investment income. Do not overlook even the smallest living expense. Without a clear picture of what you spend each month, you will not be able to realistically set an investment budget. Most people know what their main bills are and factor those expenses into their monthly budgets. But, many people tend to either forget or ignore the little things, which can add up over time. Some factors that can send your books into disarray include the following:

- Quarterly and annual bills, such as insurance, memberships, and warranty fees

- Magazine subscriptions

- Eating out

- Recreation

- School expenses beyond tuition, such as field trips, lunches, and supplies

- Gifts

- Renting movies

- Cell phone overages

- ATM and other bank fees

- Parking fees

- Car maintenance, including tags, inspections, and repairs

- Clothes

- Newspaper or magazine subscriptions

- Personal hygiene, such as your favorite shampoo and haircuts

It may sound reasonable to assume that you can live on less while waiting for that big paycheck to come after selling your investment property. Unfortunately, that is often easier said than done. After all, when you have gone two years without a vacation, or the car breaks down for the third time since you invested in that must-have property, spending less may not offer the promise it once did. Be careful to be realistic when setting your living expense budget. While some people can live without a vacation or eating out for prolonged periods of time, others simply do not have the discipline to do so. If that is the case, set your personal budget accordingly and figure out your investment income from there. Otherwise, you might end up broke and miserable.

The best way to get an idea of how can you budget your living expenses is learning from an example. Take John and Beth: They wanted desperately to jump into the emerging market game. They had heard about the opportunities to make enough money to set up their retirement income for the future and were anxious to give it a try. Before even considering how much they could (and would) invest, they sat down and worked up a realistic family budget to get a handle on their current expenses:

John and Beth's Monthly Expenses	
Mortgage	$1,500
Property taxes	$500
Utilities (electric, gas, water, sewage, cable)	$800
Phone service (landline and cell)	$200
Transportation (car payment, insurance, repairs, gas)	$1,100
Food	$500
Personal care	$125
Recreation	$500
Student loans	$250
Insurances (medical, liability)	$1,300
Holidays/gifts	$200
Retirement savings	$500
Spending money	$300
Memberships	$200
Emergency Fund	$250
Total	**$8,225**

As you can see, the grand total of their standard living expenses totaled $8,225. With a monthly income of $9,400, they figured they could swing an investment expense of $1,175 per month without stretching them financially.

The next step: Figuring out your investment expenses

Once you have a good handle on your living expenses, you can move to your investment expenses. If you already own one or two investment properties, you are going to have to factor in the costs of keeping those properties going before putting aside future funds for new purchases. Do not forget to plan for all types of emergency expenses so you do not find yourself without the money to fix a leaky pipe or replace a roof at a later date.

Once you have figured out all of your investments expenses each month, add that amount to your living expense amount. Subtract that total from your monthly income, and the leftover number is what you have to invest with. For most of you reading this book, that amount will not look like much, so you will have to find other ways to raise investment capital to buy new properties. *Using other people's money is discussed in detail in Chapter 9.* For now, take a look at the money you have on hand using numerical cost analysis.

The Numerical Cost Analysis

Whether you are new at investing or a seasoned veteran at spotting emerging markets, it is crucial to invest safely, regardless of the state of the market. When you take the time to evaluate your cash flow and choose each project wisely, you increase your chance of making money over the long haul. Move too fast and invest more than you can handle, and your quest for riches will end before you ever sell your first house. Make sure that you not only have the money on hand to make the purchases, but also that you have enough in your account to cover those carrying costs for two to three times longer than you expect to hold the property. That way, if you do get stuck with a property longer than expected, you will not run into problems paying for it.

The first step in conducting a numerical analysis of your investment monies is to determine how much short-term cash you need to buy a certain property. This includes your deposit, inspection fees, and title search.

Let us get back to our investment couple, John and Beth. Once they knew how much monthly cash they had to work with, it was time to begin calculating their probable overall investment expenses. They began their numerical analysis with a list of short-term expenses, listing the required cash on hand for the investment:

- The 10 percent deposit on a $50,000 investment property ($5,000)
- Inspection fees ($300)
- Title search ($500)
- **Total: $5,800**

Once you figure out how much money you need to even consider a certain property, the next step is to calculate the cost of finishing the deal. This cost includes, but is not limited to, the sale price, taxes, closing costs, and utility hook-ups, to name a few. For John and Beth, these costs looked like this:

- Final sales price ($45,000)
- Property taxes ($1,200)
- Closing costs, 5 percent of the sales price ($2,250)
- Realty fees, 6 percent ($2,700)
- Insurance ($800)
- Utility fees ($300)
- **Total: $52,250**

Note that PMI or loan applications/origination fees are not listed here because these investors were not planning on taking out a mortgage to finance the purchase. This may not be the case for you, in which case those costs should be added here. When it came to ongoing expenses, our investors added these:

- Monthly maintenance ($300)
- Security system ($75)
- Utilities ($125)
- Taxes and insurances ($200)
- Advertisements ($50)
- **Total: $750**

With all of the expenses laid out, you can clearly see the cost of adding a property to your investment portfolio can get rather large. Once you have a clear picture of what your outgoing expenses will be, try to evaluate any income that the property may generate through rentals during your holding time. Always cushion this number with a few extra months for when the property may not be rented. After all, few places have non-stop tenants, so it is important to factor in some loss of rental income during your holding period.

Now, add up your total expenses over the period of time you think you will hold the property, then subtract any generated income. This will determine if the property is a good deal. First, ask yourself if you have the funds available to keep this property for your set amount of time without stretching you too thin financially. If the answer is yes, calculate your bottom line sales price, factoring in any sales fees, and subtract your expenses from that amount. The amount that is left is your projected income. Keep in mind that if any unforeseen expenses arise during the time in which you own the property, or if it sells for less than you projected, this amount will be lower.

Back to John and Beth: They were smart investors. They had already saved the $58,050 they would need to purchase the property, so they did not have any large carrying costs. Since their monthly costs were $750 and they planned on renting the property for $1,100 a month, they actually were set to make about $350 per month. In the 30 months they held onto the property, it was rented for 24 months, which gave them a gross profit of $3,900. Now this may not seem like much, but consider the fact that they never had to dip into their extra income money from their day jobs during their holding time. They also invested an additional $20,000 into the property for renovations and home improvements, bringing their total costs for this investment property at $78,050.

Because John and Beth made the right improvements, they were able to list their investment property for $169,000 (about

10 percent below market value) once the market rebounded. Listing the house so low below market value garnered a lot of interest, and the house sold for $191,000. That left our savvy investment couple with a $100,000 profit from the sale (after reality fees, taxes, and other closing costs). Not a bad profit. John and Beth did have to wait more than three years to make the big bucks, but their patience paid off with a big payday.

Take a good look at your own estimates. Does the final profit projections you come up with satisfy you? Is it enough to warrant the time and expenses that go into acquiring the property? If so, consider purchasing the property. If not, you may want to take another look to see if improvements can be made, the price can be lowered, or if it should be bypassed altogether. Although this is a simplistic view of a cost analysis, it is a good way to begin figuring out how much you can invest in a specific property without getting in over your head. A financial expert is better suited to run your numbers more precisely; however, if this simple formula does not offer the results you are after, it is usually a good indicator that the property is not going to generate the profits you want.

Once you know whether or not a property is worth the risk, you will need to finance it. *Chapter 8 discusses several financing strategies that will help you choose the method that works best for your investment approach.*

Chapter 7

Financing 101

The days of subprime, anything-goes home financing are (thankfully) long gone, but investors are still looking to get their piece of the fallout from the housing collapse. In the ever-changing real estate and lending market, it is essential to know what your needs and options are before making the offer on a possible investment property. Clearly, there is still money to be made in real estate; after all, it is a great long-term investment. In the current climate, however, you must be extremely careful how you finance your dreams of investing in real estate, whether you invest in rental properties or "flip" properties for profit. How you begin your journey toward becoming a real estate investor in this changing market will directly affect how successful you are in the long run.

To help determine your financing options, begin by looking at what types of loans are available, and get to know each one and how they can be used to an investor's advantage. You may be familiar with many of these loan products, but you may see them differently when looking at them with the fresh eyes of an investor instead of the typical homebuyer. A loan you would likely never consider for a personal home purchase may be the perfect fit for your investment property. The key here, as with other aspects of investing, is having the right information to make the best decision. After all, your future as an investor depends on it.

Types of Loans

If you have ever purchased a property for yourself, you know that there are many loan products available, and it can be difficult to sort through and select the option that best meets your needs. When it comes to an investment property, you will have many of the same choices but very different requirements for your loan. In an investment situation, you are not planning to be accountable for paying the balance in the long-term — you are either going to rent out the property and have your tenant be responsible for covering the loan payment, or you are going to hold onto the property for the shortest time possible before selling it again. Your intentions with the investment property are going to be important when the time comes to make a final decision in financing the deal.

The basic loan types are:

- Long-term, fixed-rate mortgages
- Short-term balloon payments
- Construction loans
- Adjustable-rate mortgages (ARM)
- Interest-only loans

Long-term, fixed-rate mortgages

Long thought of as the gold standard of mortgage loans, the fixed-rate mortgages of the 15- and 30-year varieties have many benefits for the buyer of personal or investment property. This type of loan is the easiest to understand and comes with no surprises, a plus for homebuyers. The rate, which is determined at closing, remains fixed for the life of the loan. So, if you have a $200,000 loan with a 5 percent mortgage, your payment will stay at roughly $1,100 per month for principle and interest for the entire loan.

The monthly payment on a fixed-rate loan will only go up when real estate, school, or local taxes increase, or your insurance payments on the property also go up. Principal and interest payments remain constant as the interest paid each month decreases and the amount set aside to pay down the principal increases. This amortization, or elimination of debt over time, causes the bulk of the interest to be paid in the earlier years of the loan. By the end of the mortgage term, most of your payments will be put toward the principal.

As an investor, the fixed-rate mortgage may be a good choice, especially if you are looking to invest in rental properties that you plan to hold for years to come. These mortgages generally have low interest rates, although they do tend to be a bit higher than other shorter-term loans, so be sure to carefully calculate the risk of taking on this type of loan. Having a consistent payment does work well when renting though. You will be able to raise rent on your property as housing rates in the area increase, but you will not incur an increase in your mortgage payment as you might with other loan products. In this scenario, the profit on your rental property will drastically increase as the demand for rentals continues to grow — a side effect of many people being unable to purchase their own homes in this market.

A long-term, fixed-rate loan can still be a good solution for financing even a short-term investment property that you are planning to renovate and sell. The payments may still be affordable if you are getting a good deal on the home. In the event that you are not able to sell the home as quickly as you want, you will not be stuck with some of the inconvenient changes that other loan products have beyond the initial payment period. Keep in mind though that long-term fixed loans do come with a higher monthly payment than, let us say, a very short interest-only loan. So, if you plan a quick turnover (less than one year), it may not be the right option. These loans also tend to require a rather large down payment (about 20 percent) to qualify, another downside for investors who do not want to tie up tier cash.

What to Consider for a Long-term, Fixed-rate Loan

- Would I be more comfortable with a fixed payment, no matter what happens to the market or economy?
- Can I handle the payment?
- Do I plan to hold the property for at least 5 years?
- Will I be renting the property during the holding period?
- Do I have a 20 percent down payment?

Short-term balloon loans

Balloon loans were a heavy offender in the sub-prime mortgage debacle, but they are not bad things in and of themselves. It was not the loan's fault that so many people got in over their heads with a home they could not afford, thanks to the easy payments in the short-term with this type of loan.

As the name suggests, a short-term balloon loan requires smaller payments for an agreed upon amount of time, generally five to seven years. After that time period is up, the entire balance of the loan becomes due. As you can imagine, people who used these loans to buy their dream homes (which were out of their price range) soon found themselves unable to refinance in time to escape the balloon portion of the loan. In many cases, people owed almost twice as much as their home was worth.

The short-term balloon loan can be an effective tool for investors, especially when the market in which their property lies is selling well and have no great concerns about unloading the property after the necessary improvements are made. With a little to no down payment and just the interest and a small principal payment due at the outset of the loan, the investor has more capital in hand to make the renovations to the property and the money is not tied up in a higher payment. The monthly payment on a short-term balloon mortgage of $200,000 could be several hundred dollars less than the same payment with a fixed interest loan.

The important thing to remember about using a short-term balloon loan for investment property is home value. People who played the real estate game just a few years ago got burned when the bottom fell out of the market, which is a risk investors take again when they choose to travel down the balloon mortgage path. Since emerging market investors are usually in it for a longer haul, short-term balloon loans can be risky considering a huge payment is due at the end of the loan term, and these types of loans can be difficult (if not impossible) to refinance, especially in a weakened economy, so be sure you can handle the large payment at the end if you are unable to either sell or refinance at that time.

Did You Know:

In 2004, condominiums accounted for more than a quarter of all multifamily construction in the United States, according to the National Association of Home Builders.

Construction loans

Construction loans differ from the previously discussed mortgages because they cover the building process rather than an actual property. The amount of the loan is disbursed as needed to cover the costs of building a property; thus this type of loan is often referred to in the mortgage and lending business as a "story" loan. It comes by its name because the bank is essentially buying into the "story" of your plan to build. The bank takes your word (and credit and collateral, of course) that you will complete the job and make the payments.

During construction, only interest payments are due on a construction loan, and the interest is due on the money that has been paid out. If you are building a $200,000 home and have disbursed $100,000 of the money, you will be paying the interest on that. Most construction loans "come due" when a certificate of occupancy is issued for the property, at which time the loan can be converted to a standard type of mortgage.

If you own the land on which you are building property, this works in your favor in the financial way of not only spending money on a building lot, but also that it will be collateral to help secure construction financing. Problems arise, however, if property values fall during the building process, since the loan must be paid in full when construction is complete; not when you sell the property.

What to Consider to for a Construction Loan

- Do I qualify for a construction loan?
- Do I plan on reselling this property as soon as the building phase is complete?
- If I plan on holding the property after construction ends, am I in a position to refinance into a regular mortgage?
- Is this property likely to maintain its value (or increase its value) once it is completed?

Adjustable-rate mortgages (ARM)

Similar to the short-term balloon payment mortgage is the adjustable rate mortgage (ARM). This has an initial period — possibly two to seven years — with a lower payment, after which the interest rate and payment increase sharply. Often these loans begin with a "teaser" rate, which, depending on the circumstances and the credit worthiness of the borrower, could be as low as 3 percent.

Once the initial period has elapsed, the rate could go above the prime rate, rendering the payment unaffordable without refinancing the loan. This reset put a lot of people in trouble in the sub-prime lending market just a few years ago when they realized that their home's value had not increased and they could not simply refinance the mortgage to avoid the increase in interest. This was another way that the real estate "game" backfired for a lot of people without the continued increase in home values.

The advantage of an adjustable rate loan for the investor is two-fold. As with the balloon payment loan, the initial payments are low. This keeps expenses down and more cash in your pocket when you need it to make improvements and renovations on properties you want to resell or rent out. Additionally, homes are at rock bottom prices in many markets and have nowhere to go but up. If you are buying in a bottomed-out market, it stands to reason that you could hold onto the property for several years without worrying about refinancing the mortgage. By the time the loan is scheduled to reset, the home should have gained value.

The cons of using this investment strategy is the fact that these loan types generally feature a larger (and sometimes even unreasonable) interest rate after that low-interest period has ended, which will mean larger carrying costs and less profit for you. With mortgages so difficult to refinance in a sluggish economy, you just might find yourself stuck with those growing payments for years.

What to Consider for an ARM

- Would very low payments be helpful in keeping my carrying costs down?
- Can I handle the higher payments once the initial low-payment period ends?
- Do I know what my payments would rise to as the interest rate rises?
- Can I handle those payments if I am unable to refinance the loan later?
- Do I plan on selling this property within 1–3 years?

Interest-only loan

If you think of loans as a family, the interest-only loan would be a first cousin to the ARM and short-term balloon loans, as they share many common traits. As its name suggests, the interest-only loan has an initial period where the borrower only pays the interest on the loan, with nothing paid toward the principal. This makes it a good choice for an investor looking to buy a property to renovate and then sell.

It did not make good sense for the millions of people who got into properties they could not reasonable afford by using this type of loan. As with those who over-financed homes with other types of teaser loans, those people who had paid only interest for a year or two found themselves unable to afford the much higher payment they were forced into when their loans reset to the full amount.

The actual payment on an interest-only loan runs roughly 15 percent less than the payment on the same loan with a fixed rate and a 30-year term. Of course, this type of loan requires paying a higher interest rate, and you likely have to pay private mortgage insurance that goes along with financing the whole amount of the property. If you want to hold onto a property for the long run, an interest only loan is unlikely to save you any money; thus, it may be more of a hassle than any savings would be worth. Plus, you will not be able to earn back any equity on the property during the holding period, which will mean you will have to garner a higher selling price in order to justify your overall investment costs.

We are in a very different housing market than we were just a few years ago and the inflated prices and bidding wars are gone and replaced with foreclosed properties and bargains. Choosing the interest-only route may only help if you are looking for a quick resale.

What to Consider for an Interest-only Loan

- Am I short on cash for a down payment?

- Am I planning to sell this property before the interest-only period ends?

- Can I handle the larger payments if I am unable to sell the property in time?

- Am I in the financial position to refinance the loan later?

- Can I still make a profit if I do not build equity in this property during the holding period?

Qualifying for an Investment Loan

When you are looking for a mortgage for your personal residence, the procedure is relatively straightforward — a credit check and the verification of your income is all it takes to get your money. When the property in question is going to be used as an investment rather than a residence, the process is different, yet similar. Instead of determining if you can afford the mortgage based on your salary, the bank will want to see your plan for the property and whether you have the collateral and credit to back up your dreams of investing in real estate.

You do not need to double your income before you can afford a second property. What you do need is a plan for making an income from the property that will back up why you are investing in that type of property. The first loan will probably be the toughest to secure; after all, you are asking the bank to take a chance on your business skills and investing plan. Once you have one successful investment property under your belt, you will look much better to the bank for subsequent properties.

151

Your loan will be classified as non-owner occupied (NOO) and will be subject to different rates and fees than that of a typical owner occupied property. The interest rate for a NOO mortgage will be higher than the same loan for a primary residence.

The ripple effects of the housing market collapse are still being felt throughout the industry and are affecting borrowers and lenders alike. At the height of the market, an investor could buy a property with little or no money down because the risk to the lender was very small. When a home could double or triple in value over the course of a few years, the banks had very little to worry about when writing loans. Putting money down — 20 percent or more — will lower your interest rate significantly because investment property mortgages are based on the loan-to-value ratio (LTV) of the property. That means that the more you can put down on the home, the better. If you are putting 30 percent down, you will get a much better interest rate than if you are trying to swing a loan with no money down. This is especially important for the new investor who does not have a successful reputation on investment rental or resale to prove to the lender.

Three Cs of Borrowing

Credit scores are important to everyone in society: Your car insurance company keeps track of your score to help determine your risk as a driver, a prospective employer may run a credit check before hiring you, and your lender will be checking your credit score to assess your suitability as an investor. But, there is more to credit than just a number — there are the three Cs.

Character

Character may sound like an old-fashioned term to be using to refer to your credit worthiness in the realm of real estate investing. We are, after all, well past the time when you could take out a loan based solely on your personal relationship with the banker or with just your good family name as proof that you will pay back your loan. Your credit score, however, is a snapshot of character, especially as it relates to how you treat your obligations. Your score, as you probably know if you are considering jumping into the real estate investment market, is essential to your ability to borrow money, and it depends on many factors.

Your credit score is a number that defines you, and it is made up of many factors that all contribute to this picture of who you are in relation to meeting your financial responsibilities or not. Your character as defined by the lender is important because it is a barometer of risk. They are shelling out a lot of money and want to make sure that the person they are lending it to will pay them back. They will look into your credit history to do that. To review, the factors that affect credit are:

- The type of credit you use = 10 percent
- New credit you have been given = 10 percent
- The length of your credit history = 15 percent
- How much you owe, and its proportion to available credit = 30 percent
- Your payment history = 35 percent

Based on many factors, a credit score is a long-term, well-rounded picture of your character to help the lender make their decision. Because this simple number is vital to your chances for successful real estate investing, you must make sure that your credit score is correct before you get started with the loan process. You do not want to find out that there are mistakes on your credit report when you have already found the perfect distressed property and need to make an offer that same day. Do your homework and understand your score to improve your presentation of character to the lender.

Capacity

As the name implies, capacity refers to your ability to pay back the debt. Of course, that is all the bank has in mind; they do not care if you are a well-liked person, or even if you have a sharp business mind. They want to see evidence on paper that you have the means to pay the mortgage you want. Just as you would get approved for a certain amount of money based on your salary and expenses when applying for a mortgage on a primary residence, you will have to prove that you can meet this obligation to the lender. The bank will likely want proof of:

- Employment, namely your stability at a job, not that you have job-hopped for 10 years
- What kind of debt you currently carry
- Your living expenses
- Your number of dependents

Collateral and capital

This is really two Cs, but they are closely related. Many people mistakenly think that collateral is the money that is put into the house, but when making a purchase, collateral is the house itself. Sound confusing? People tend to think of giving collateral to get a loan. For instance, if you need money, you can put your car up for collateral and borrow against the car. In the event that you do not pay back the loan, your lender would be allowed to repossess your car. The car would secure the loan for the lender. In the case of mortgages and other *secured* debt, the lender has the right to take possession of the property in the event that you do not make the payments as scheduled in the mortgage paperwork.

So, in the case of the real estate investment loan, the bank will want to ensure that the property is worth the amount you are financing. After all, they are going to get the property if you do not fulfill your commitment to paying back the loan. With housing prices in a constant state of flux, the idea of collateral may be hard for banks to swallow. What the home was worth last month may not be what the home is worth in six months, but the important thing is that the loan you request is not for more than the value of the home in this ever-changing market.

The flip side of this C is capital. Essentially, this makes sure you have the finances to back up your plans. There are plenty of variables when it comes to lending, and the amount of money you need to have is one of them. It will depend on your credit score and associated risk to the lender, as well as the value of the property and the amount of the loan you are requesting. The bank will look to see that you have assets beyond your salary, that if you were to lose your primary income, you would still be able to maintain a second property.

This is why it is easier to finance a second or third property, or even more than that. Your income from these properties can back up the payment for your newest addition. If you are just getting into the investment market, you will need to have money in the bank or other investments to shore up your plan. Many first time investors have trouble proving that they are up to the task of buying and investing in real estate and turn to others for help with investing. However, it is possible to invest on your own if you want to.

Investment Capital: How Do I Get It?

If you have been doing your research on the housing market, you may think 2010 is perfect time to jump in and start buying properties, especially distressed ones that can be scooped up for a fraction of their previous value. Unfortunately, it is also a time when banks have become wary of lending money and want to see a significant amount of stability in their prospective lenders. As discussed, the days of financing just about anyone for whatever they want are long gone, and have been replaced with a conservative strategy that will likely be better for everyone in the long run.

Investment capital is the money you have "in the bank" so to speak, when you go to a lender to request a loan for an investment property. You will probably be putting money down on the property, especially if you are a new investor in real estate. You are also going to have to show that you are "good" for the debt, meaning that you have something beyond a paycheck to count as assets toward paying back your loan. Take a look at some of resources you have for investment capital:

Credit cards

You probably had one of two reactions to the term "credit card:" You either thought something along the lines of, "No way would I use a credit card to help purchase a property," or a light bulb went off and you thought, "I could definitely use a credit card to get this started." Your reaction is important because this idea can be risky and, for many people, using credit cards can spiral into other financial problems. Contributing to the risk of using consumer credit to help fund a purchase is the recent legislation and correlating changes in the ways credit card companies are handling their customers. Restrictions have tightened, even for those with excellent credit who pay their bills on time. Credit card companies are well aware of the increase in bankruptcies and foreclosures and know that they stand to lose millions before it is all over.

Take all those points into consideration. If you still feel that you can handle the payment on the investment property, plus the considerable payment for the loan on your credit, then it can be done. Many people, especially during the height of the flipping craze, were able to carry out lucrative deals using only their wits and a few credit cards. They could sell a home in a matter of months — what was another $10,000 on their credit card, especially when their profit could be up to 10 times that amount? In this new standard of real estate, investors need to look at the bigger picture of their property purchases, so use of a credit card should be taken very seriously.

Home equity

There was a time when using home equity, either through a loan or by cashing out equity in a refinance, would have been a great way to purchase a property for investment. With low, tax-deductible interest on the loan and stable home prices, using the equity in your current home was simple and cost effective. The same factors that have created the surplus of distressed properties and record-low housing prices across the country will have most likely affected your home and made it difficult to access and use your equity.

Of course, this depends on your circumstances. If you have owned your home for many years, you may still have plenty of equity to tap into. You may even own your home outright and can draw on its value to get the working capital to make a real estate investment. In those cases, using the money in your home still affords the benefits recently discussed without greatly increasing your risk.

If, however, you have recently purchased your home, you may find that you have little or no equity available. Many homeowners are dismayed to find that even after faithfully paying their mortgages for years, the housing crisis has left them with little to show for it. Some are even "upside down" in equity, meaning they owe more on their home than it is worth in the current market and do not even have the option to tap into their equity.

Savings

Dipping into your personal savings to fund an investment is a mixed bag that heavily depends on your financial stability. If you have significant savings, it can be a safe and easy way to get in the door of investing. You have $25,000 in savings and only need $5,000 to get the property? Great, the bank will be thrilled to see your application. If you have the same amount in the bank but need $22,500 for the down payment, things might not run as smoothly.

As mentioned earlier, the first investment property is the hardest to obtain. Even if you already have a property, the bank may not take any rental income into account for your assets until you have two years of history. Banks always look out for themselves. You could have the best investment plan, but if you do not have the financials to back it up, you will have trouble getting it off the ground. For your own peace of mind, consider how much you would need in savings should you or your partner lose your job due to layoff, illness, or other circumstances. Also consider keeping an emergency fund for the new property in case there are delays in selling or renting it.

For the smart investor — and having a good chunk of money in savings qualifies you as a smart investor — personal savings can be a great way to open the door to real estate investing. Having your own starter funds will help you through the loan process without putting you under the gun once you have started investing. Knowing you only owe the mortgage is a great feeling, since you will not incur extra debt from borrowing the down payment for the property.

The risk is the only downside to using your own savings, but risk is almost inherent in investing. In this volatile economy, most of us are at risk of losing jobs or are facing a decline in family income that could be detrimental to our lifestyle and well being. Risk is always involved in purchasing an investment property, but there is also long-term stability in owning real estate. The important thing is to weigh the risk against the benefits.

Retirement funds

You may be of the opinion that you should never mess with your retirement account. That can be true, depending on how close you are to retirement. What many people do not realize, however, is that investment property can actually be purchased using funds from your individual retirement arrangements (IRA) without any tax penalty. (Read: The property must be an investment property. This means you cannot purchase your own residence with funds from your IRA, but you can use that money to get started in real estate investing.) It may even be a safer bet than the stock market.

There has never been a better time to get deals in the housing market, and with an eye on a long-term investment in an emerging market, your IRA funds could be your ticket to wealth and financial stability. There are areas of the country that have seen a drop in housing prices of over 75 percent, such as California, Arizona, and Florida, as well as a drop in home purchases. Therefore, renting a property for a time with the intention of selling when the market picks up (all the while collecting lucrative rents) is a solid long-term plan.

When you are using IRA funds to get into real estate, there is yet another tax break. If you sell the home and roll the profits back into your IRA, you will not pay tax on the money you make from the sale of the home. With unrest in the stock market, people are looking into real estate for a little security, and they are right to do so. Historically, there is no better investment than real estate in the long run. The days of buying, flipping, and running are basically over in most parts of the country, with the new investment strategy being all about identifying the right market and making long-term decisions on how to proceed. Your IRA could be the perfect resource to get you started in real estate investing.

Creative Financing Solutions

The way you choose to finance your investment property is essential to the success or failure of your endeavor. Just as important as finding the right property is securing the right financing for your dream of investing in real estate, and there is plenty to consider when making those decisions. It is a good idea to map out your goals and worries so you can meet both of them head-on, knowing exactly where you stand and what changes to make to achieve your goals and overcome the concerns that crop up along the way. In addition to the traditional types of mortgages already examined in this section, there are many creative financing options worth investigating to see if they are a good fit for your particular situation.

Seller Financing

Seller financing is often thought of as a last resort for someone with bad credit or who has gone through a bankruptcy. In our new standard of real estate, things are much different, and a seller may finance a property for a buyer under several circumstances. If the property is uninhabitable in its current condition, the seller may agree to finance the transaction so it can be sold. Traditional mortgages generally cannot be written for homes that cannot be lived in — for example, if they have no kitchens or bathrooms. Also, if the home has been for sale for a long time or the seller is desperate to unload it, as is often the case after a death in the family. If you choose to enter into a seller-financed deal, it is important to continue to seek representation. Because a mortgage is still a complicated document, you need to ensure that your needs as the buyer are being met and your interests are protected.

Lease/purchase Agreement

A lease/purchase agreement is rare in a seller's market, but these are increasing in popularity in today's uncertain climate. Essentially, a lease/purchase agreement allows a buyer to enter into a lease contract with the option to buy the home at the end of the lease period. Each month, a portion of the rent is designated as a deposit that will eventually become a portion of the down payment on the property. If the renter/buyer does not want to purchase the home at the end of this period, they forfeit the deposit and are not obligated to buy the property. As the buyer of an investment property, you can implement a lease/purchase agreement. This installs a tenant in the property who covers the cost of the rent during the lease portion of the contract, and then purchases the property when it becomes available at the end of the lease.

Secondary Mortgages

The practice of taking out two mortgages on one property was essentially unheard of slightly more than a decade ago, but with the explosion in the housing market that caused prices to skyrocket, the 80/20 loan was born. The secondary mortgage does more than provide 100 percent financing. It also effectively eliminates the need for the buyer to purchase private mortgage insurance because the main loan (the 80 percent) considers the second loan to be the equity, so it does not require the Private Mortgage Insurance (PMI) to be paid. As it pertains to investment property, a secondary mortgage may help you get started with investing. However, take care to ensure that you have the means to pay the entire mortgage amount and that the rent you will collect on rented properties will cover both mortgage payments.

Government Grants

Grants from the government do exist, but they have a mythical quality. Everyone seems to know someone whose second cousin got a grant for a particular thing, but there are also scams out there. The government grant program is an option for investors willing to do their homework to find the money and apply for grants. If you choose this route, be cautious that you do not waste time and money on Web sites and books that make more promises than they can deliver.

Mortgage Assumption

A mortgage assumption is an agreement where the buyer simply acquires the payments on the current mortgage. It can be a great arrangement for both parties if the conditions are right, but it can also be a logistical nightmare unless professionals orchestrate it. You can make a mortgage assumption work in your favor with good representation.

Owner-occupied Rental

If you are purchasing a multiple-unit property, the possibility of an owner-occupied rental is a great way to get a good rate on what is essentially an investment property. The catch here is that you do have to occupy the property. If you already own a home, you would then have to rent your own home out and move into the new property, because your mortgage would be considered owner occupied. (Committing mortgage fraud is a federal offense.) If you do not yet own a home and want to cash in on both the buyers' market and the investment bargains, this is a perfect way to get started. You would simply be purchasing your home with rental units on the side.

However you decide to finance your investment property, make sure to do your homework so you know you are getting not only the best deal, but also the most fitting loan for your needs. You may plan to own and rent out several units in one building, or you might buy properties to renovate and sell. Whatever your plan and your needs, there is a financing option that is right for you.

CASE STUDY: FINANCING TIPS

Jorge Newberry, investor

Financing can be intimidating and confusing for a new investor, but having a good understanding of the way real estate investing works and how it differs from financing a personal property is essential to success. Seasoned investors understand the system and have learned that entities, such as limited liability companies (LLCs), are the way to go for large-scale investing. Jorge Newberry learned this lesson all too well throughout his years of investing and has put his experience to work to help families avoid foreclosures.

Newberry uses a combination of LLCs and singe-asset entities to purchase larger properties, taking advantage of the personal protection this financing provides for the investor. When he purchases a property, he anticipates that everything is going to succeed, but experience has taught him to prepare for the worst-case scenario. At one time, he owned more than 3,000 units spread out over dozens of buildings in several states and concedes that at some point at least one of them would have a problem. Using the single-asset entity protects not only your personal finances but the other properties as well.

Newberry relates one example of how real estate investing can be different than you expect, and the way you finance the deal can make all the difference. After purchasing and moving into a troubled property in Columbus, Ohio, his mettle and resolve were tested as he fought crime rates and Mother Nature to try to save the complex. He was able to renovate and revitalize the apartment complex until an ice storm damaged the apartments beyond repair. Although his personal finances were strangled during the height of the crisis, he was able to rebound from the loss, thanks to the entity ownership he uses with his large purchases. The loss of Woodland Meadows did not affect his other properties and holdings.

Working with a real estate lawyer to develop the LLC or single-asset entities is a great way for a new investor to employ the self-preserving tactics that experienced investors use over and over for large and small investments. After learning valuable lessons about crisis management and resolution, Newberry has continued to try to make a difference for other people with his program for homeowners who are facing foreclosure.

Chapter 8

Using Other People's Money

Investing in real estate may seem like a dream to you, especially if you lack the funding to get started, but it does not have to be that way. Finding an investment partner, whether that is a rich family member or a commercial bank, can be the path to the real estate investment and wealth that you have been hoping for. Essentially, any non-cash transaction is a form of using other people's money (commonly abbreviated as OPM). Anytime you take out a loan, for instance, you are using the bank's money to make a purchase you would have been unable to make yourself at that time. A credit card works the same way: You are able to purchase something instantly even though you do not have the cash in hand.

When it comes to investing, using other people's money is a little different. Imagine if your kids came in one day with a plan for a lemonade stand. They found the perfect location with plenty of traffic, it is a hot summer day, and there are yard sales up and down the block. What they need from you is investment capital. Without your financing, they cannot get the lemonade, the cups, or the ice to start their business and rake in the profits. If you say yes, you have just become an investor in their idea and they are using OPM — specifically, yours.

Keeping Face in a Gloomy Economy

Do not be put off by the economic downturn in late 2008. Many seasoned investors look at a downturn as a gold mine, rich in opportunities for those who dare. A downturn may be where you begin to build your empire. It may surprise or inspire you to know that many great companies got their start during challenging economic times, including IBM, HP, Hershey's, Texas Instruments, and Microsoft. Challenging markets can spawn incredible innovation and creativity. By using OPM, you can launch your business idea to service a sector of the market that has a need for which you have a product, or you can begin investing in real estate to fulfill your dream of renovating homes. In return, the person whose money you are using will also benefit. Maybe they will earn money from their investment in your enterprise. Or, maybe they will own a stake in your business. With risk comes the potential of great reward, and that is what OPM is all about — for both the dreamer and investor.

Excerpt courtesy of *Using Other People's Money to Get Rich* by Desiree Smith-Daughety

What is OPM?

Financing your real estate investments deals is certainly not the same as asking your parents for some start-up cash for a lemonade stand, but the concept is similar. You have the idea and the know-how, but you do not have the money to put your idea into practice.

The real difference between using OPM through investors and using OPM through a traditional mortgage is the way the investor is paid. When you take out a mortgage to buy a property, the lender makes money on the interest payment on the loan. The lender will never make more than what is laid out in the original mortgage document because he or she is paid on the mortgaged price of the home. If you purchase a home now for $150,000 and take out a mortgage, the interest will be paid on that amount, even if the home's value triples over the course of the loan. With investment OPM, the lender owns a piece of the investment, a stake in its success.

This difference is even more important when it comes to securing investment capital for your real estate investment. Your source of OPM is looking to make money off your investment plan, not from the interest paid on the loan. Accordingly, the process and approach to finding investors is different from those used for securing a mortgage on property. The mortgage company looks to the property and its value to determine the risk of loaning you money to make a purchase. An investor, however, looks to you and your plan to determine whether you and your business plan promise a good return on investment.

OPM for real estate investing

The most obvious benefit of using OPM for your real estate investment is that you do not have to put up your own money to close a deal. You can keep your own cash reserves while generating wealth for yourself and your investor. In a perfect world, you do the scouting and the investor fronts the cash for the investment. When the property stars paying off, you both reap the rewards. Some people have the money to invest in real estate, but neither the time nor the desire to do the work necessary to broker deals, handle repairs, or manage tenants and collect rent in the case of rentals. An investor will be more than happy to sit back and collect on his or her investment, while you put deals together and do the work.

Another benefit of OPM is timing. If your cash flow is waning, but you have a lead on a great property and have the knowledge to put it together and make it profitable, an investor of OPM could be the fuel for your fire. You do not have to miss out on an opportunity because you do not have the funds available. Leveraging your resources and having OPM as part of your investment arsenal is a great way to keep projects in play at all times. One of the marks of a successful real estate investor is always having more than one property in progress. Rather than depend on the success or failure of just one deal, you can be making several deals at once without sapping your own finances.

The ability to diffuse the risk is the final benefit of using OPM. When you bought your home, you signed the mortgage and promised to pay back the loan or face foreclosure and repossession of the property if you failed to make payments. In an OPM situation, you share the risk with your investor, so you both take on the responsibility if things do not go according to plan. You must address this risk in your business plan, so that you can both find and investor and have a strategy already in place should things go wrong. You will want your own interests and those of your investor to be covered in the event of failure.

The drawbacks of using OPM

Before discussing the drawbacks of OPM, it is important to note that without this type of capital investment, few deals would ever be made. After all, when you do not have the money in your checking account to pay for a home, you do not just shrug your shoulders and walk away; you head to the bank and apply for a mortgage, using OPM to finance your dream of homeownership. Without mortgages, few people would ever be able to buy homes. The interest you pay to the bank is well worth the ability to purchase property.

Just as you pay interest on a traditional mortgage, using OPM to fund real estate investing also has a price tag. The exact terms of the agreement with your investor will vary, depending on the amount invested and the deal you broker with them. Sometimes, inexperienced and enthusiastic investors will sign away too much of their own deal to their investors, leaving them disappointed with their profit margin. Understanding how to negotiate with an investor is essential to setting up a mutually beneficial arrangement for both parties in the transaction. You will not make as much money on a deal worked out with OPM, but it is worth it if the alternative is to not make the deal.

Keep it Legal

Your relatively small real estate venture may not seem like a big deal, but many investors unknowingly break Securities and Exchange Commission (SEC) laws. The passive nature of the investment in the property, meaning that the investor is merely providing the funds, makes, it a security. Having an experienced attorney draw up and approve all paperwork will keep your transaction legal and help you avoid any trouble.

Depending on your investor, another drawback could be loss of control on the project to a certain degree. As mentioned earlier, some deals are written so that one party has more control than the other. In other cases, an investor may try to exert control over the details of the project. This can be typical of both venture capitalists, who want to make money and do it quickly, as well as your Uncle Joe, who thinks you should put window boxes on all rental units in the building he helped you purchase. Deciding to seek and use OPM means giving up a modicum of control, so be careful to construct the deal according to your desires and take friendly advice with a grain of salt. You will not be your investor's employee: You will be his partner.

Once you have taken all variables into consideration, OPM is a great way to open doors in real estate that would otherwise remain closed. The benefits of investors sharing the risk and providing the necessary capital for your property investment outweigh the minimal drawbacks involved, as long as you have a solid investment plan.

Sources of OPM for Real Estate Investing

When you find the perfect investment property and realize you do not have the cash flow to make it a reality, it can be disheartening. The smart investor, however, will take this as an opportunity to think outside the box and find the capital to make those dreams come true. It is not as simple as opening the phone book or searching OPM online, but it may be easier to get started than you think. Here are the best places to start your search:

- Inner circle
- Outer circle
- Professional investors
- Banks

You may already be brainstorming and getting the ball rolling about asking someone you know for money, but first let us take a look at each type of investor and what they can (and cannot) do for your real estate investment plan.

Get it in Writing

Whenever you enter into any kind of financial agreement, it is essential to have the entire thing in writing. A good contract will protect your interests if the project fails or if your investor tries to pull out before the project is complete. If you are taking money from family or friends, a handshake may seem like enough of a contract, but it is not: Always get it in writing.

Your inner circle

Experienced real estate investors may balk at the idea of combing your friends, family, and close business associates for OPM, or they may admit that they got their start that the same way. When looking to start a new and possibly lucrative venture, your family or closest friends and associates can be a great resource. After all, they want to see you succeed, and if you do they will be included in your success. What could be better than getting rich and taking someone you know and care about with you down that road? Your inner circle can be a great resource for investment capital, but there are some considerations when getting into business with family and friends:

- **Are they investing in you or the plan?** Family members, friends, and associates are less likely to check out your business plan. Oftentimes, they feel like they know and trust you and want to help you succeed. While this can be very encouraging, it can also mean that you do not have to present them with a solid plan. Skipping that step can be disastrous — having someone else scrutinize your plan is often the double-checking you need to be sure you have chosen a good investment.

- **Are you getting it all in writing?** When going into business with a personal contact, it is vital to have everything in writing and to be sure that both parties understand the ramifications of the investment and plans. The consequence of misunderstandings in the case of using OPM from family members may be more than just the loss of capital: It could mean the loss of a relationship.

Treating an investment from a family member or friend in exactly the same way you would treat that investment from a bank is your best insurance for the deal. Developing and presenting a business plan and detailing both the investment and the exit strategy will ensure a smooth investment with a member of your inner circle.

Your outer circle

When it comes to finding sources of OPM, networking could be your new best friend. Some people find networking troublesome or even dread the thought of it, but viewing networking from a different perspective may be all you need to get started. If you think of networking as attending a party or social event where everyone wears a nametag and spends the night introducing themselves to each other, it is no wonder you may avoid it altogether.

Rather, think of networking as a natural, organic occurrence. Remember those old shampoo commercials where "she told two friends" and so on, until the entire TV screen was covered with little squares of people? Well, that is networking. Getting the word out about your investment opportunity can be the spark that ignites your search for the OPM you need to get your project off the ground. Today's networking can be done with social media like Facebook and Twitter, or it can be done the old-fashioned way through word of mouth.

All investment opportunities are subject to the laws of the Securities and Exchange Commission (SEC). Its objective is to protect consumers from predators who offer faulty or fraudulent investment opportunities. Using networking in your favor can help you avoid the pitfalls that can come from cold-calling people you want to invite as investors. The wider your outer circle of friends and contacts, the more people you will come in contact with. Finding OPM for your project is a numbers game — increase your numbers, and you increase the likelihood of finding a favorable investor.

Professional investors

If you are just starting to investigate using other people's money to finance your real estate endeavors, you may be pleasantly surprised to find that there are professional investors just looking for the right place to put their money. These investors generally fall into two categories: venture capitalists and angel investors. The type of investor you seek depends heavily on the type of project you are pitching and how much of an investment you are asking for. On the whole, venture capitalists are looking to make a large amount of money quickly, while angel investors may be more satisfied with a smaller return on investment.

Be Prepared

This book has stressed the importance of being prepared. When you are approaching a personal contact, an angel investor, or a venture capital firm, you must have your project ready and your business plan in hand. The better you represent yourself and your investment, the better your chances of getting some OPM.

Venture capitalists

Venture capital firms can be likened to a mutual fund, with many investors putting their money and faith into a firm that will invest the money for them. Rather than pitching your idea to an individual person, you will package it for a firm of investors represented by a few people who handle new investments. Being prepared down to the dollars and cents is essential if you seek funding from a venture capital firm for your real estate endeavor. Investigating the firms choosing one whose goals match yours increase your chances of getting the funding you need. If you simply pick a firm out of thin air and pitch your plan, you will probably not be a good match. Some firms have rigid formulas and restrictions, and you will be denied if your proposal and financials do not meet their standards. Remember that rejection is not personal with venture capital firms — it is because your project did not meet their requirements or worse, because you did not present it well enough to gain their confidence.

If you intend to purchase and renovate a block of apartments and turn them into residential and office spaces in a mid-sized city, look for a firm who shares your goals and vision for that city and project. Aligning yourself with their mission statement and giving a thorough, detailed presentation are the best ways to impress a venture capital firm and get the OPM you need to get started.

Angel investors

So named because the money they offer seems to come from heaven, angel investors can be the saving grace for new and seasoned real estate investors alike. In the emerging market sector, this group of investors plays an important role in the revitalization of communities across the country. Angel investors differ from venture capital funds because they are wealthy individuals who have more freedom of choice when selecting investments. They are often characterized as giving from the heart, rather than from the bank. All investors want to hear your story; they want you to convince them to put their money on you and your project. Angel investors are even more interested because they may have interests of their own. Beyond the potential to make money, name recognition is a powerful motivator for angel investors. Because they may already have the finances to cover your investor, angel investors look to make a national, well-known difference in their investments. This could be an important cause, a newsworthy business opportunity, or getting into a more creative career.

Networking to find investors can lead to many types of angel investors, especially in the markets that have been hit hard by a recession or unemployment. If you have plans to breathe life back into a favorite city or hometown, that angel investor will pull out the checkbook before you have even finished the presentation. Having the right story certainly puts you ahead of the game, but you still have to be prepared to show the project's viable and financial information. While an angel investor controls of his or her own finances and may not be looking for the high return that venture capital firms do, he or she will still want to be investing in a solid plan. A good story without the expertise to back it up will not get you far in acquiring OPM for your investment.

If an angel investor sounds too good to be true, you will not be surprised to find that there is a catch. Just as venture capital firms are out to make money by fronting the money for your real estate project, so are angel investors. Because angel investors are willing to give seed money and take a chance on start-ups, they absorb more risk than their venture capital counterparts. They may have a different timeline in mind for a return on their investment, but they will likely want a big chunk of yours. Angel investors often look for a cut of 10–50 percent of the property, which could leave you without the controlling interest of your own project. This demonstrates, again, the importance of getting everything in writing. Giving up a hefty portion of your investment may be worth it if you are just starting out or the opportunity is too good to pass up. Either way, having every stipulation clearly written out is essential for the success of a partnership with an angel investor.

Professional investors have what you need: money. On the flip-side, you have what they need: a great plan for making more money if they support your project. If you can get your plan to the right investor, you will be well on your way to making OPM work for you in real estate. A good relationship with an investor will lead to more opportunities for both of you. If you work well together and you produce good results for your investor, he or she will be likely to fund other projects or refer you to other contacts for more investment capital. As mentioned earlier, the investment process is largely a numbers game, so go in prepared and keep going until you get the answers and money you want and need.

	Venture Capitalist	Angel Investor
Organization	Formed by a group of investors who pool their resources to make a profit	Wealthy people making investments individually
Size of investment	Large-scale investments that are usually over $1 million	Small-scale investments that are usually under $1 million
Focus of investments	Interested in helping investors expand once they are off the ground	Receptive to start-ups and new investors looking for smaller amounts of capital
Expectations	Focus on emerging business and expect quick, substantial returns	More likely to accept a steady, slower rate of return for a new investment

Banks

You may not think of banks as a source of OPM, but they are the most popular and commonly used of all the sources. A mortgage behaves in much the same way as the other types of OPM that have been discussed — it affords you the ability to obtain something that you do not have the available cash to purchase, you immediately get what you want instead of waiting until you have the money saved, and, finally, you owe the lender something in return for the benefits you are receiving.

Banks not only make investments in the form of mortgages but in investment loans as well. The major difference between OPM from the bank and from a private investor is that the bank will charge interest on the loan instead of taking a portion of the project. They assume a portion of the risk, but require collateral from you to secure their investment.

Business Plans for your Real Estate Investment

One of the most important factors in successful investing is preparation. Throughout this book, you will find that being prepared and understanding all the variables involved in each step of the real estate investing process is essential to a good outcome. Many people have lost money in real estate because they moved impulsively and didn't consider the consequences of their actions. Of course, preparation will only secure an already sound investment, but it cannot be stated strongly enough: The better prepared you are, the better your chances of success.

When searching for a source of funding, you must develop a business plan. You might not think that your real estate investment project is a business, but it is. You also need to present your proposal in a professional and thorough manner to prospective investors. They will not give you the funding you need on just a hunch or good idea. Anyone willing to give you their money wants to see exactly where it is going and how you plan to make them a profit and pay them back.

As mentioned earlier, you may be tempted to skip this essential step when seeking OPM from your inner circle. Do not give in — make sure you do all the necessary work to present a comprehensive plan. Even if the investors are not interested in the details of your plan, it will help solidify your ideas and give you valuable practice developing a business plan. As you expand your investments, you may be called upon to present a professional business plan, so that experience will serve you well.

OPM and You: Tips for Success

- Have a back-up plan
- Do not get discouraged by rejections
- Hire an attorney to protect your interests
- Exude confidence even when you are not feeling it: investors hate desperation
- Have a realistic timeline and be patient with it
- Do not count your chickens till they hatch — you do not have the OPM till all the paperwork is signed

Business plan basics

Business plans range from outlines to volumes, with everything in between. They all share some common characteristics. Generally, business plans are made up of four sections: description, marketing, finances, and management.

The written part of the business plan should include a cover letter and a statement of purpose, which can be tailored to your specific needs. If you are seeking OPM, you can package your business plan for the interested investors and address your cover letter directly to them. Taking the simple format of a business plan and making it fit both your goals and your actual proposal can be a very eye-opening experience. Certainly, when you put a plan together, any missing pieces or flaws in your plan become obvious. Do not be discouraged if this happens — better to find out that your profits will not be what you want before you obtain OPM for the project. Doing the research necessary to get your business plan in place can help you avoid major headaches later on.

Obviously, the descriptive part of your business plan should detail everything about the project you want to fund. The more information you can give to your would-be investors, the better. Package the details and write them in a positive way, paying special attention to items that would be of interest to your source of OPM. If you are trying to get an angel investor excited about a project that is in their hometown, make sure you stress how important the building is to the local community and what it would mean to have it renovated and restored for family and small business use. Similarly, if you are pitching a huge apartment complex deal to a venture capital firm, they will want to know the condition of the apartments and how much work needs to be done. Your description can often make or break both the business plan and the hope of obtaining the OPM necessary to achieve your goals.

As it pertains to real estate, the marketing section illustrates the local real estate market and how your property stacks up against the competition. Showing your project as a viable option in an emerging market puts the odds in your favor with investors. If you find that you cannot compete in the local market, consider it a red flag about the project and reassess the deal as a whole. Marketing also encompasses your plans to rent or sell the property once you obtain ownership, and how you will handle that portion of the transaction.

Once you have captured your investors' interest with your summary, you have to impress them with your financials. While several financial categories deal with speculation or projected profit and loss, you cannot afford to make mistakes.

Do not overestimate profits to impress your investors, or you will find yourself in a bind when your project cannot live up to their expectations. It is better to be turned down a few times with the correct numbers than to be unable to produce what you said you could. Even if your project has a modest profit outlook, you may still be able to find the OPM to do it.

The financial section includes both how much OPM you need to seal the deal, as well as how you plan to make a profit with the property once you have it. You can also include your offer of terms for your OPM source in your business plan. While they may make a counter-offer, you will at least look like you have done your homework in that area.

When it comes to writing

Now that the basic categories of the business plan have been covered, here are the basics of writing one. There are many variations of business plans, depending on specific needs and the purpose of the plan. When writing a business plan to obtain OPM from prospective investors, the audience and their particular concerns should always be taken into consideration. The Small Business Administration's Web site, **www. sba.gov**, is a great resource for all things related to business plans. It also offers examples of plans that you could tailor to accommodate your project and its needs.

Once you have all your facts in place, you can start to package your proposal in a manner that is well thought out and makes the best impression on your investors. Here is the breakdown of what to include in your proposal.

- **Executive summary:** This section should include your objectives, company mission statement, and keys to success.

- **Market analysis summary:** This section should detail the housing market in the area where you are investing in property. It can also explain how you plan to rent or sell the property.

- **Implementation plan:** This section details how you plan to take your investor's money and complete your project so that it will show a profit.

- **Sales strategy and projection:** This section explains what the plans are for the property, both short- and long-term. If you are planning to rent out units, that should be included here.

- **Projected profit/loss:** This section may be the hardest for new investors and you may need to get help to complete it because it may be difficult to estimate how much you will earn.

- **Financial plan:** This section outlines how you plan to pay for the property and its renovations, if necessary. It also explains how investors will be included in profit sharing.

- **Management summary:** This section explains your role in the project. If you plan to be hands-on during the whole process, include that here. If you are sub-contracting the work, include that, too.

- **Summary:** At the end of your plan, you should wrap it up just as you introduced it at the beginning.

Where to go for help

If you are new to investing and have never seen a business plan, the whole process can be intimidating. If you have been investing for a while, you may be familiar with how to make a profit and loss projection or a management summary, but even a seasoned investor can use help when putting together a presentation for OPM. Oftentimes, the reason you need OPM is because you could not otherwise close the deal, so your business plan can make the difference between success and failure.

The Small Business Administration is a great resource, both through their Web site and local chapters, for anyone needing help with a business plan or other aspects of getting started in business. There are also many examples of business plans available on the Internet to show you how other people have set up their plans. If you have an attorney, he or she can be an invaluable resource in setting up your business plan. Accountants can also help with the financials, which are vital to the success of the plan. There are even software programs that will walk you through the entire process of completing a business plan for the proposal to your investors.

OPM and
Your Investment Success

Ask any successful businessperson how they got successful, and they will likely share one thing in common — they have all sought others' help when they needed it. Whether that means hiring a contractor to put a roof on a property or enlisting the services of a Realtor, the thriving real estate investor knows when to delegate and when to seek out the resources he or she does not have. Looking for sources of money from other people is the same thing. Many people feel unable to seek funding for projects or feel that they have to wait and earn it themselves. That could not be further from reality. Angel investors, venture capitalists, and banks make their money on the ideas and hard work of other people. They have the capital you need to get your idea and investment career off the ground. Tapping into those resources is a smart business practice, and can get you from a beginning real estate investor to a comfortably success-ful real estate investor faster than you could have imagined.

SECTION IV:

What to Do With Your Property Once You Have It

When you secure your finances and transfer the deed, you have officially begun investing in real estate. Now the real question is what to do with this property that you have already spent so much time in securing. The first step in making money off your real estate investment is to increase your property's value so you can sell it for more you paid for it. Because you will most likely be renting out your property while you wait to sell in order to offset some of the carrying costs, you will need to be landlord. If this is your first time owning a property other than your primary residence, this can be a difficult trade to master.

Chapter 9

Increasing Your Property's Value

Your goal as an emerging markets specialist is to make as much money as possible without expending a lot of work or energy in the process. There are plenty of ways to increase a property's value simply and easily — not to mention cheaply. The key to figuring out what needs to be done is through understanding what the market requires. You do not have to figure this out alone; there are some tips and techniques other professional investors employ to ensure that their properties appeal to the most buyers and get the highest possible sales price.

Establish an Action Plan

Every new property acquisition is an opportunity to take a diamond in the rough and bring out its full brilliance. This requires action, and no action is possible without a solid game plan. If you want to succeed in emerging real estate, you have to be able to do more than see the potential in a property; you have to figure out a way to bring that potential to the surface. Your action plan will help you do just that.

Your action plan must first list your overall goals for the project. With these goals always in mind, establish a list of action steps to help you reach your goals in a timely manner. This is not the time to think conservatively. Although you want to spend as little money as possible, you also want to create a plan that will work. This may take a bit of creativity and out-of-the-box thinking to get you the most bang for your buck. That may include planting a beautiful garden in the backyard, adding a washer/dryer on the first floor, or having the house professionally staged to show potential buyers how splendid it can look with the right furniture and accessories. None of these things cost an arm and a leg, but they can help to increase buyer appeal when it comes time to sell.

Of course, your action plan may include projects that are much more detailed and expensive than these simple fixes, which is why knowing what you are up against is so important.

Accentuate the positive

The first step in showcasing what your property has to offer is to accentuate the positive. Many things can attract a buyer, but nothing generates interest like unusual architectural accents like unique moldings, staircases, doorways, and fireplaces. If you can find a property that features these hard-to-find accents, make them stand out with the right paint, décor, layout, and more. Do whatever you can to make potential buyers take notice.

Maybe your newest acquisition is a rather small home but has an amazing yard and is situated in a budding neighborhood. Use those benefits to attract buyers who may otherwise not even consider a home of that size. You can almost always add on square footage, but you cannot always find a pleasant and safe neighborhood that is close to schools, parks, and other amenities. Make every effort to help potential buyers see these benefits.

If your investment property features a small kitchen, but an oversized deck or back porch, use that to your advantage. Turn the extra space into another living space to help offset the negatives of the kitchen. The trick here is to make potential buyers fall in love with one or two things within the house and help them overlook those things that may be a stumbling block.

Get caught up on maintenance projects

Maintenance left undone can make a property look both shabby and uncared for: two things that can wreck a sale. Buyers want to feel confident that they are buying something that has been taken care of so they do not have to worry about unforeseen problems cropping up. Taking care of the simple things, like adding a fresh coat of paint throughout and shampooing or replacing the rugs altogether is fairly inexpensive, yet can make the difference between a "For Sale" and a "Sold" sign hanging in the front yard.

Take the time to carefully look through each property you buy and make a list of maintenance projects that need to be taken care of. Fix all of the cracked or broken windows and replace old and worn-looking fixtures, doorknobs, and pulls for a fresher, newer look. A fresh coat of paint and new hardware in a kitchen or bathroom can have a dramatic effect on how new the room looks.

Fix all squeaky doors, make sure that no faucets leak, and ensure that toilets flush properly. These are the things that can make or break a potential sale.

Pretty things up a bit

Once you have fixed all big and small maintenance issues, it is time to pretty things up a bit. Again, you do not necessarily have to spend a lot of money. The key is to make the house stand out in small ways. People nowadays like impressive-looking front doors, so adding one to your home can increase its curb appeal.

Installing specialty light fixtures can also go a long way to increase interest. Fixtures are a great and inexpensive way to add warmth and character to a single room or an entire home. Sure, a lot of people are adding granite counter tops to their kitchens and bathrooms these days, but that can be rather pricey. Opt instead for ceramic tile or engineered stone that could be a fraction of the cost of granite. Or, try something totally new in hopes of offering a more unique flavor to the house. Try not to get too trendy here. Simple is more universal and cost effective.

There are a lot of small touches that you can add to a house to give it more buyer appeal. Try adding a rocking chair to the front porch or a stained glass window to one particular window — anything that will get noticed and say "one of a kind" to a potential buyer. Uniqueness sells but so does simplicity. Strive for a balance in both and you will create a home no buyer can resist.

Decide What To Do To Make the Most Profit

It can be easy to get carried away when you are trying to improve a property and make it more salable. But remember, this is an investment and you want (no, you need) to make a profit. So, choose your improvements and upgrades wisely. Opt for those that are most needed or will glean the most benefits. You may think that adding an atrium-type room to the back of the house would be lovely, but if what it really needs is a second bathroom, spend the money on the bathroom.

Styles and tastes change, so be wary of adding things to a property that are trend-oriented, unless you can do it fairly inexpensively or the house simply will not sell without it. A few years ago you could not get a certain price for a home without stainless steel appliances. In the years to come, there will be some other trend that requires a change before you can sell a home. Just be careful that the changes you make are indeed what buyers want and are willing to pay top-dollar for. Otherwise, you might waste a lot of unnecessary money.

Another danger to watch out for: making upgrades and improvements in accordance with your personal likes, dislikes, and preferences. While you may love a lot of bold color, most experts agree to create a neutral space that any buyer can enhance to make their own. Maybe you would not dream of owning a home unless it featured wall-to-wall carpeting. That may be beautiful, but if the market requires hardwood or laminate with area rugs, you had better forgo your own flooring preferences and opt for what sells. Far too many new investors purchase cupboards, flooring and other accents in accordance to what they would want, never thinking about what others like. Usually, the more universal the upgrade, the cheaper it is. You may want all high-end appliances in your own home, but if your investment property does not need more than midline to sell, why spend more than you have to?

Improve the property's economic use

There may be a time when you come across a property that offers some sort of extra amenity that can be enhanced and used to increase its economic use. This is good for the community and it is great for your bottom line.

For instance, an apartment complex that features a large pool area may be a financial hardship to the complex owner, unless he or she decided to open the pool up to the community in the form of paid memberships. This allows the residents to belong to an exclusive club for free (thus raising the rent potential) and bring in some extra income to the owner through seasonal pool memberships. Another example might be the purchase of a larger farm. In many situations it is possible for the investor to sell the farmhouse, barn, and other outbuildings with a few acres and subdivide the rest of the farm for single homes. Some investors may go as far as to build the new houses themselves to make more money, while others simply sell off the lots to individual buyers who want a custom build.

For example: One savvy investor, Jim, bought a fixer-upper home that featured an adjacent lot. He put a few thousands dollars into fixing the house and sold it for a small profit. His bigger profit came later when he built and sold a new construction home on the lot. While the original house paid for the investment and made maybe $10,000, the sale of the next project brought in the real profit — more than $150,000. Another investor may not have seen the profit potential in that lot and sold it with the original house.

The point is to always be on the lookout for ways to improve a property's economic use to make even more money than you would on just the land or house alone.

Increasing the value of your property may be as easy as improving its efficiency. Oftentimes, many homes are over-assessed, which means that you are paying more taxes than you should. It can be a hassle to get a new tax assessment done and will cost you at least a few hundred dollars for the application and appraisal costs, but if it lowers your overall tax bill your bottom line will improve. Better yet, when you go to sell your investment, it will be more appealing to potential buyers when they compare your house's tax bill to a neighboring home that is for sale.

Insurance is another place where you can often save. There are several ways to cut your insurance bill for yourself and future owners: add extra smoke detectors, an alarm system, and a sump pipe. Most of these cost-cutting measures do not do much to lower premiums when used alone, but when added together, some homeowners can experience a 25–50 percent savings.

Use marketing to your advantage

Never underestimate the power of a great marketing plan. Whether you are marketing a property for sale or for rent, knowing how to generate interest is the key to increasing profits.

One of the most ingenious marketing ploys used recently in the real estate industry was a seller who put a $300,000 appraised property up for auction with a starting bid of $10,000 and a guarantee that the highest bidder would walk away a homeowner — no matter what the size of the final bid. This was a risk, but this seller was marketing savvy and went above and beyond the norm for marketing this sale. He put up posters, took out newspaper and radio ads, got an interview on a local morning TV show, and even sent college students door-to-door to several area apartment complexes to drum up interest. On the day of the sale, so many people showed up that the local police force had to handle traffic. Bidders from all over the state arrived, ready to buy a cheap house. Auction fever took hold, and the property eventually sold for more than 20 percent higher than any local sales comps suggested it should. Not only did the seller walk away with $40,000 more than his original asking price, but he also enjoyed a quick sale and was not required to pay any sales commissions. His marketing plan worked.

There are many ways to use marketing to your advantage when selling your investment properties. This is just one example of how thinking outside of the box can bring in profits. Whatever marketing plan you use, be sure that it is memorable so people remember the property, your company name, and company logo in the future.

Time Your Improvement Projects

Every property can use some type of improvement or renovation to make it more appealing and able to bring in a better price when it comes time to sell. Make certain, however, that you do not do those renovations too soon. You may be anxious to upgrade a property right after you purchase it, but if you are planning to hold onto it for any length of time, you would be better served to wait and see what the market requires when you go to sell. This way you know you will not waste money putting in tile floors when the fad suddenly changes to hard-wood. By the time the current market rebounds people's tastes and needs will likely change, and you will want to be prepared to offer your potential buyers what is fresh and new — not what was "in" two, three, or four years earlier.

When it comes to increasing your property's overall value, there are a variety of methodologies to try. The mistake many new investors make is trying to incorporate all of these value-increasers into their investment strategy. Not only will this cost you more money than you will get back, but it will take more time and energy than you want to spend on your property. Be careful when picking and choosing improvements for a specific property. Always gauge the probable return on this extra investment to determine if it really is worth your time, energy, and money. Sometimes it may be worth selling a home for less money than to try and fix it up for just a few thousand more if it entails a lot of extra effort that would be better used finding your next property.

When not to invest more in a property

Not every property can — or should — be improved. Other than cleaning it up and making it look a bit fresher, some homes simply are not worth the added expense of renovating. Here are a few situations when you should leave your investment property as-is and try to make a quick sale:

When a neighborhood suddenly begins to slide: Neighborhoods usually do not quickly become dangerous or uninviting, but sometimes they do (or you miss the earlier signs of trouble and get stuck with a house in an undesirable area). In the event that an area in which you hold investments suddenly hits the skids, the best strategy is to leave the house as-is; slap on an irresistible price and unload it quickly. Renovating a home in a poor neighborhood is not going to entice a reluctant buyer: It is just going to cost you money.

When the house already contains the right amenities for the neighborhood: Buyers may want the best looking house on the block, but they are not usually willing to pay well above the neighborhood pricing cap for it. It does not matter whether your property has high-end appliances and fixtures — if other houses in the area are not commanding your asking price, the odds of you getting it are slim. Despite what many sellers may think, there is a cap to what you can reasonably ask and get for your house. If your investment property already offers the same types of amenities as others in the neighborhood, be careful not to over-renovate, or risk losing those costs. For instance, adding granite countertops or a third bathroom to a home in a neighborhood where all of the houses have Corian® counters and two bathrooms may interest buyers, but it likely will not bring in a higher sales price.

When the market is on its way down: During a cycle downturn, the worst thing you can do is spend money on a property just to get a higher price. When prices are falling, they continue to fall regardless of what improvements are made.

When a neighborhood has hit its peak: Even if prices are not falling, if you recognize that a certain neighborhood has hit its pricing peak, be careful when making improvements. Stick to the ones that are necessary to make a sale, but keep your cost as low as possible. Adding those special touches now will not command a higher price; what they will do is make your home more appealing to buyers.

Chapter 10

Are You Ready to Be a Landlord?

Most people who have paid rent have thought about being a landlord. It seems simple enough — just buy a property and find someone to live in it, then sit back and collect the rent check every month. If you've been on the renting side of that equation, you know rent is not cheap and you may be feeling like your landlord made a lot of money from you. With distressed properties in abundance and mortgage lending tighter than it has ever been, it is a good time for investors to get in on the rental market, as long as you know what you are getting into.

Maintaining and renting multiple rental units can be much more work than a beginner investor is prepared for. Below is a step-by-step look at what is involved and how you can determine your own personal readiness for this investment before you head out with a real estate agent to find properties. Being a landlord takes specific skills, patience, and persistence, but if you have those you can make your investments work for you and build wealth.

Choosing the Right Property

We are in a particular market right now that is near flooded with available properties, but how do you choose the right type of property that will attract good, stable tenants? Assessing the local market is just as essential when you are choosing a rental property, as it is when you are looking to acquire a property you plan to renovate and re-sell. Just as people will be looking to purchase a home in a safe area with access to jobs, trans-portation, shopping, and other amenities, renters will seek the same things. If a local area has lost all its jobs, it will not be a good place to purchase a property to rent.

College towns are a great place to purchase a rental property, but many investors shy away from this type of rental because students may not be the best renter. The damage they inflict on properties and the high turnover rates make this type of rent-ing problematic even though it can be very profitable.

Applying the standards for emerging markets that have been discussed throughout this book will also help you find a solid rental property. Remember that your prospective renters will need to work and shop near the property and will be looking for schools and other resources in the surrounding areas. With foreclosures happening at an overwhelming rate, there will be many former homeowners who got caught up in the mortgage crisis and forced into rental situations. They are looking for homes for their families and kids, and your rental property may be just what they need.

Why Use a Property Manager?

Many landlords do all the maintenance, rent collection, and problem solving, while others rely on the help of a professional property manager for these day-to-day issues. Most investors agree that when they find themselves owning many rental units, a property manager becomes a necessity. Others will advise to hire a property manager with your first rental property because doing so will free up your time to pursue other investments and leave the details of the rentals to someone else. What you decide will ultimately depend on what you have in mind for your properties.

First, let us look at what property managers do. While services may vary, most managers offer all of these services: repairs and maintenance, yard work, rent collection, evictions, and vacancies. If you have not yet researched becoming a landlord, that list may be surprising. But, if you are going to be ready to get started renting out properties, you need to know all that is involved. An experienced property manager will have the expertise in all these areas and will be able to present you with a contract detailing all of their policies for the services they provide. Property managers generally handle minor repairs and maintenance on the rental units, with the exact terms of repairs decided in your contract with them. The property owner often sets up an account to be used for funding repairs under a certain dollar value (say, $400). When repairs are necessary in excess of that threshold, the owner must be contacted before any work is done.

Also essential to finding a good property manager is determining what kind of communication you will be using. If your properties are a good distance from your home, a property manager can be an invaluable resource for you and your tenants, as long as you have good communication. Having an experienced property management team can make the landlord feel like a "hands off" investor, but you do still need to stay dialed in to what is going on with your property. The more you know about what your manager is doing, the better your experience will be as a landlord.

As you narrow your search for a property manager, you will want to ask specific questions about his or her services, and be sure to communicate your own needs as the property owner. Let them know how involved you plan to be with the property and what you expect from them. Also, find out how much of the repairs, landscaping, or other work they will be doing themselves and what portion they will contract out. Most property managers charge a percentage of the rent, from about 5 percent to as high as 20 percent, depending on the services they provide. Of course, you will want to find the best quality managers at the best possible price, so do not be afraid to ask for and call references. Establish all terms up front so you have all the information you need to make the best-informed decision you can. After all, the success of your rental will lie in the hands of your property manager.

If you decide that you do not need a property manager after all, just know that you will be the person getting that midnight phone call when the furnace stops working. You may even find yourself mowing the lawn at your rental unit when your lawn guy does not show up.

Who is Your Perfect Tenant?

Every investor has a horror story to tell about at least one tenant. From pets gone wild to crazy evictions, there can be a lot that goes wrong when it comes to renting out properties. But, the one thing that seems to plague landlords is lack of maintenance of the property or excessive damage that exceeds the security deposit the tenant paid when he or she signed their lease. How can you find good tenants that will pay the rent and keep the property as nice as if they owned it? Unfortunately, it is not an exact science, but there are things you can do to increase your chances of finding good tenants. Take a look at what the qualities of a great tenant are:

- Pays the rent on time every month
- Takes great care of the property
- Does not have lots of pets
- Feels invested in their neighborhood
- Stays long-term
- Communicates with landlord when problems arise

Sounds great, right? You may think you just have to find that exact person, but there are things that you can do as the property owner that will help to attract this type of renter and keep them happy for the long-term.

If you were selling a home, what is the first thing you would do? Obviously, you would make it look appealing and be sure that everything is working and ready for someone to move in. It may sound simple, but doing these same things when it is time to find tenants can go a long way toward finding the right kind of tenant. If you are renting a single home, paying attention to the landscaping and curb appeal of the home will attract a family who wants a place they can call home. If you are renting out student-type housing, giving it a home-away-from-home atmosphere will help you find the right type of renter.

Next, consider both the content of your ad and where you will place it. If you are renting a property out in your local community, try bulletin boards at community centers, daycares, and churches before putting it in the newspaper. You will find people who are already invested in the community. Word your advertisement so that the property sounds appealing to the type of tenant you want to attract, paying special attention to community or local amenities. Using personal references and contacts to find tenants can be a mixed bag. Although it may be a good way to find quality renters, it can also be more difficult to deal with a tough situation when you have a personal connection with your tenants.

When it comes time to select a tenant from a pool of applicants, ask for and check references, run credit checks on the candidates, and even ask for paycheck stubs and W-2 forms from their jobs. You can also decide to charge an application fee that would cover your costs of running credit checks (be sure to consult your local laws about how much you can charge and whether or not you have to refund money). Just the assumption of a credit check will naturally weed out people whose credit is bad because they generally already know what their credit report will show.

If you do the work to find good tenants, it will pay off with huge rewards in the long run. Having tenants who fulfill those qualities listed above will make your property owning and renting experience simple and lucrative. There are no guarantees when it comes to tenants, but you can tip the scales in your favor to having good ones.

The Price is Right

Setting a price for your rental property can be tricky in a fluctuating market, but it is something you should consider before you sign the paperwork for the property in the first place. The rent must cover the obvious expenses, such as the mortgage payment and taxes, but it also has to cover all the incidental expenses that will crop up over the term of the lease. The main expenses that the rent must include are:

- Mortgage payment
- Taxes
- Homeowner's association fees
- Property insurance

Some of the less obvious expenses that must be calculated into determining the rent are:

- Vacancy fees
- Upkeep
- Repairs
- Property management fees

Do not worry if your head is spinning right from all the information; it just takes careful planning to set the right price for your rental. Here is a hypothetical example.

Expense	Amount	Total per month
Mortgage	$1,000 per month	$1,000
Taxes	$2,400 per year	$200
Homeowner's Assoc.	$1,200 per year	$100
Vacancy	1 month reserve ($1,000)	$84
Upkeep/repairs	2 months reserve ($2,000)	$168
	Subtotal	$1,452
	Property manager fees	$140
	Total (before profit)	**$1,592**

As you can see with this example, you are looking at almost $1,600 in rent before you have figured in any profit for yourself. If the market will bear $2,000 a month for your rental, then you have a great property on your hands and can look forward to a good profit each month. If rentals in the area are running closer to $1,500, then you may want to keep looking for a better property. Of course, factoring the upkeep and repairs into the monthly rent payment will give you the necessary reserves to fix problems that arise. If there are more problems, it will eat into your profit; if there are fewer, you will have a surplus.

The rental market is essential in pricing your property effectively, and you will have to do some detective work to find out how your rental unit stacks up to others available in the area. Unlike home purchases, many of the little luxuries you might want to add to your unit will not give you a great return on your investment with rental income. Most people have the eventual goal of owning their own home, which naturally creates a ceiling for rental prices. There is a very small percentage of tenants who are willing to rent a luxury property — keeping it simple, modern, and clean will help you set a good price for both you and the tenant.

The discussion keeps coming back to the market, and for good reason. If you have a property that you think is great and you have renovated it with extra attention to detail, you may feel that it is worth $2,500 in rent. Unless the market agrees with you, it does not really matter what you want to rent it for. In a depressed market, you will not be able to rent your property for top dollar, which is why it is essential to figure out the market before choosing a property in the first place. No one wants to be stuck with a great rental unit that loses $500 a month. It is better to do your detective work before the sale to ensure the best chance for a good return on investment in the long run.

Making it Legal

Specific laws relating to tenant/landlord relations vary from state to state and even between local municipalities, but there are some standards that all landlords need to consider before they begin looking for tenants. The three main areas of tenant/landlord obligations deal with finances, maintenance and safety, and access.

Understanding what your rights and responsibilities are within each of these categories will help you avoid major headaches down the road and keep the lines of communication with your tenants open and positive. Nothing is worse than unpleasant surprises for either party when issues arise, so careful planning will help you prepare for whatever lies ahead.

Financial

Although your entire contract with your tenant is based on finances, there are certain issues that pertain to rentals that you need to familiarize yourself with. Security deposits, generally in the amount of a month or two of rent, will nearly always be collected at the lease signing. These deposits do not actually belong to either landlord or tenant. In most cases, the funds are held in an interest bearing escrow account in the names of both parties.

Your rental agreement or lease, along with local and state laws dictate exactly how the funds are to be held and how they can be used by the landlords to cover expenses, either from failure to pay rent or from damages beyond normal wear and tear to the property. Generally, the landlord can deduct expenses for repairs from the security deposit at the end of the lease period. A pre-rental walkthrough of the property is a great idea for both parties' peace of mind. After a good inspection, you and your tenant can agree upon the accepted condition of the property and avoid disputes about damages when the lease expires. Security deposits, minus any necessary deductions, need to be returned to the tenants after they have legally vacated the property.

If you are employing a property management company, they will likely handle the bulk of the pre-inspection for you, as well as the collection of security deposits. Check with them to see how they handle security deposits and what your role in that process will be. This is another area where the expertise of a property manager can save you valuable time and energy.

Another financial consideration is property insurance. You may be able to require your tenants to secure renter's insurance to cover their personal property (if you cannot require it, you should at the very least strongly suggest it), but it is your responsibility to insure the property. Your mortgage company will require homeowner's insurance, and you may also be paying PMI as part of your mortgage package. In the event that you do not owe anything on the property, you still should keep property insurance to cover your own assets.

Maintenance and safety

Again, laws vary from state to state, and individual cities often have laws that govern the habitability of dwellings. Some towns and cities consider basement apartments illegal. Others just closely guard against the misuse of property to avoid slum-like conditions, in which too many people live together in a particular home. In some areas, there are laws barring opposite sex children from sharing a room in a rental unit. Obviously, it is a good idea to consult your attorney or property management company about the specific laws governing rentals in your area because some may be obscure.

Whatever the particular laws, the underlying obligation for the landlord is to keep the unit safe and in good working order. If you have rented a unit with appliances, it is your responsibility to ensure that they are working and to replace them if they break. If your unit was rented without a washer and dryer, your tenant is responsible for obtaining and maintaining them.

Your rental agreement or lease with your tenants will allocate responsibilities such as minor repairs, utility payments (unless you have decided to include them in rent), and exterior regular maintenance, such as snow removal or lawn care. Many landlords will require that tenants are responsible for repairs under a certain financial threshold – perhaps $50 so the tenant can make these him or herself. This alleviates the need for the landlord to make the repair or to pay for it, and allows the tenant to quickly take care of small things that crop up during the rental period. Your lease can also include terms that address intentional damage done by residents or damage that occurs as a result of neglect on the tenant's part.

If you are employing a property manager, maintenance will be high on the list of responsibilities for him or her, so you should be clear about their policies and requirements for maintenance. A property manager can be especially helpful with maintenance situations when you live far away from your rental unit and would need to travel to assess damage and make repairs.

Access

Once you have given your tenant the keys to the property, it technically is not yours in the same way anymore. You are still the owner and legally responsible for the dwelling, but the law views the tenant as having certain rights. Most states prohibit the landlord from entering the property without notifying the tenant first. This law protects the privacy rights of the tenant because, as the landlord, you do own the property, but you do not own the belongings within.

In most cases, there is some provision in the rental agreement or lease for emergency entry without notice. The amount of notice and reasons for entry, such as showing the unit to a prospective tenant, doing maintenance, or replacing items, should be detailed in the rental agreement or lease so that both parties understand what is allowed and expected. If a tenant refuses your right to enter as detailed in the agreement or alters the locks so that you cannot enter the premises, you have a legal right to recourse.

Again, in the case that you are employing a property manager, all details would include him or her as an additional party who has access to the unit. The property manager would be acting on your behalf and the lease would reflect that status with the company.

Rental Agreement versus Long-term Lease

Often used interchangeably, the terms lease and rental agreement actually refer to two different things, and the distinction will be important to your success as a landlord. When the perfect tenant was discussed earlier, one of the best qualities they could possess was the desire to stay in your property long term. A lease is a long-term contract with standardized terms that legalizes the agreement between a landlord and a tenant. A rental agreement is similar, but is generally written with monthly renewing terms and does not provide the same type of protection for the renter that a lease will.

A rental agreement will be used in the case of a short-term rental, typically less than a year and sometimes for as little as a month. The terms of the rental agreement are usually such that it renews itself unless one or both parties terminate the agreement. The landlord has the right to change the terms of the agreement as he or she sees fit. In contrast, a lease agreement will be used for periods of a year or more and is better for both parties. The benefit for the landlord is the assurance that he or she has a stable tenant for the duration of the lease. The tenant can rest easy in the knowledge that the terms of his or her lease will not change, and he or she will not be forced out during that time period. A termination clause is generally included in both types of agreements with the details of how each party can end the agreement, usually with either 30 or 60 days' notice.

Because of the expense of turning over the property for a new tenant, as well as the possibility of having an empty unit between tenants, it is preferable to keep tenants as long as possible. The draw for you is that, even though you cannot raise the rent during the terms of the lease agreement, you also will not be incurring the additional expenses of cleaning the unit, advertising it for rent, or getting hit with the loss of income while your property manager is getting it ready for new tenants. In the case of finding a great tenant, keeping them for two years is worth more than the possible 10 percent increase you might add for a new tenant after that first year.

Another way to convince tenants to sign a long-term lease is to offer some type of motivation on the anniversary of their rental. Maybe carpet cleaning or repainting a room or two are enough incentives for your tenants to sign a longer lease or renew the one they currently have. This saves you money in both the short and long term because you are doing a little extra maintenance before that tenant moves out, and you are preserving a great lease agreement while avoiding extra costs.

You can hire an attorney to draw up your rental agreements and leases, or you can just walk into your local office supply store and buy one off the shelf — but those are the extremes. If you have been working with a property manager, they will likely have standard rental and lease agreements that they use and are familiar with, so that is a great choice. If not, check with your real estate attorney or Realtor for more information on where to get your agreement. Whichever type you choose, always get it in writing. Many people rent to family members or friends without a lease agreement, but if you are really interested in being a successful investor, you should keep it all business. The agreement should address:

- The amount of rent
- The date rent is due and to whom
- The length of the agreement
- Who is responsible for paying utilities
- Whether pets are allowed
- Whether the tenant is allowed to sublet the unit
- How many people are allowed to occupy the unit

In addition to these items, the lease should detail how any dis-agreements or disputes will be handled, up to and including missed rent payments and eviction procedures. Evictions vary from state to state, and your lease agreement should reflect the most up-to-date laws of your jurisdiction to protect both your interests and the rights of your tenant.

Subleasing contracts

Allowing a tenant to sublet a property is usually more trouble than it is worth, and may even be prohibited in some areas that have rent control laws. When you are just starting on your career as a real estate investor and a landlord, it is probably best to keep things simple and learn how to find good, reliable tenants who will pay on time, without getting into allowing your tenant to turn around and rent out their obligation to you. Of course, there could be extenuating circumstances, such as a family emergency or illness that make subletting a possible solution, but those should be considered only on an individual basis and not be built into the lease agreement. You are in this landlord game to make money and to protect your interest. Opening up the door to subletting only puts your investment at greater risk.

If you have made it this far without skipping to the next sec-tion, you are probably ready to face the challenges of being a landlord. As with anything worthwhile, becoming successful at renting out your investment properties will be the result of preparation and hard work and will definitely be worth the trouble.

SECTION V:

Beating the Bust

Eventually in the real estate investment process, there is going to be a time when you have to decide when you should sell and finally earn a profit for all the work you have done. This is a matter of making sure you have reached your investment goals, as well as making sure the current market is suitable for a sale. Once you have determined it is time to let go, you will be taking on the opposite role from when you first started investing in emerging markets. You are now the seller, and your main job is pricing the home right in order to turn a profit.

Chapter 11

To Hold or To Sell

If there is one thing that successful house flippers learned in the early 2000s, it was to get in and get out as quickly as possible. While this may have been a solid investment strategy when prices and demand were high, a shift has been made in recent months, leading more and more investors to make plans for keeping their investments for a while to reap higher profits later. Patience is the name of the game, and those willing to sit on their investments for a few years will likely be the big winners at the end of this endurance race.

How long you ultimately hold onto your investments depends on your own circumstances, the local real estate market, and how much money you want to walk away with in the end. With nowhere to go but up, those in a position to wait out the current real estate slump can — and likely will — make a bundle if they handle their investments correctly. It is not always easy to know when to hold onto a promising property, let alone when to get rid of it, so this chapter will help you build a winning hold versus sell strategy.

Establishing Your Goals

The first thing you will need to figure out before deciding whether to hold or sell is how much money you want to make on a specific property. What is your bottom line profit? Is it possible to sell now and meet this goal? If so, then by all means, list your house now. But, if there is no way that the market can sustain the price you need to ask right now, be prepared to hold onto that property for a while. When determining what your final profit can and should be on a property, consider these important factors:

- What sales price both good and bad markets can handle. If you need to walk away with a $25,000 profit on a house and the current market will only reap a $10,000 profit, consider what price a house in a better market will bring. Maybe holding your investment for two years can increase your profit potential to $20,000 or even $30,000 — is it worth the hassle of keeping it for the extra money? If the answer is yes, then hold.

- The outlook for the area. Keep a close eye on the neighborhood after your purchase. If things keep looking better, hold for as long as you can to make the most profit. But, if something unexpected comes up and the outlook for this emerging market suddenly takes a downturn, consider getting out while you can.

- The ability to make some money on the property while it is being held. If you find a good tenant and can rent the property for enough to cover your carrying costs, then you should consider holding it until prices go up.

After all, why shortchange yourself by settling for less than you should now, when you can hold out for bigger profits later?

- What improvements to put into the property. As we have already discussed, there are a lot of things to consider when making improvements on a property. Sometimes the kinds of improvements necessary to bring the best price on a home will help determine how long you hold it. For instance, if you plan to add a master suite, the odds are you will have to hold the property for several months or longer until the construction is complete. If, on the other hand, you just plan on making some minor aesthetic fixes to the house, you will not have to factor in construction time into your hold/sell strategy.

- Your ability to cover all of your costs. If you find yourself in over your head financially, you may need to consider unloading some of your lesser profit potential properties to safeguard your better investments. Be sure to keep a close eye on your bottom line to avoid unnecessary risks.

Where Your Property Stands in the Timing Cycle

We have already discussed the importance of real estate timing when it comes to buying property; now consider the place of the timing cycle when trying to sell for the most profit. You wanted to buy your investments when the timing cycle was in a downturn to get the best price. Now, you want to watch for those natural upswings to bring in the highest sales price and profits. Here are a few things to watch for when determining when to stop holding and begin selling.

Buyers: You cannot sell anything if no one is buying. That is why it is important to watch for signs that buyers are returning the market, but not just any buyers. You want the quality buyers who will be willing to pay your price. Just because there are a lot of sold signs going up in an area does not mean that you are ready to sell yet. Check to make sure that the prices those houses are selling for meet your profit analysis goals. A big mistake that some new investors make is putting their investments on the market too soon. They notice an upsurge in sales and assume that the market is turning around, when in reality it is more investors jumping aboard. Certainly, they would not be entering the market if things were not looking like a turnaround was near, but why sell off too early and let other later investors make the big bucks? Oftentimes an upsurge in sales happens a few months before an actual price increase as other investors begin to see a turnaround and jump into the market. Do not fall for this fake turn-around. Now is not the time to sell too low to another investor who will reap the big profits in a few months. You have held out this long; hold onto your property long enough to reap the real market upsurge.

Financing: Be sure that you do not list your property before financing options return. Otherwise, you may find yourself struggling as buyers put in bids on your properties without the financing to back them up. This is not only nerve-racking, but it can make your property look bad if future buyers see that there have been multiple offers on your property and no sale. They may walk away thinking there is something wrong with the house, not understanding that it was simply buyer-financing that squelched the deal. Be sure to watch for signs that banks are lending to average buyers again or some new buying incentives, like government tax breaks, are being offered to entice a new set of buyers into the market.

The neighborhood outlook: Do not wait for a neighborhood to hit its peak before putting out that for sale sign. The best time to sell is while a neighborhood is still growing and people want in. You may make more if you wait, but it can be much more difficult to sell in a peaked neighborhood as buyers flock to the new up-and-coming area instead.

At the opposite spectrum is not recognizing when a neighborhood is on a downward slide. Watch for signs that people are moving out of an area and sell as soon as you can if you think that your area is next.

Signs to watch out for

Foreseeing a market downturn may sound like randomly predicting the future. On the other hand, with unemployment rising and home prices slow to rebound, it may seem ridiculously simple. But to be honest, it is somewhere in between. While the market continues to fluctuate and change — and even economists are not truly sure how things will work themselves out — there are some warning signs that investors can look for when they are trying to locate investment properties. Seeing the signs and understanding them can help you to make the most informed decisions about where to invest in properties and what to do with them once you have bought them.

When housing prices were going up people were reluctant to face the fact that they would eventually have to come down. In markets like California, New York, Nevada, and Arizona, home prices tripled over the course of nearly a decade, which is way above the historical trends for home price increases. Few people heeded warnings of the bubble that was about to burst because nearly everyone was making money: the banks, the brokers, and the sellers. Buyers were paying high prices, but thanks to creative financing, they were not feeling the real pinch of their purchase until the bottom fell out. Unfortunately, for some that was too late.

So, aside from using a crystal ball, how can you tell what the market is going to do? One way is to keep up to date with what the big mortgage companies are doing. Fannie Mae and Freddie Mac announced in 2007 their determination to what they call "declining markets." In order to protect their mortgage investments in these markets, buyers have to provide twice the down payment normally required for the same loan. For instance, if you were hoping to purchase a $250,000 home in Washington, D.C. with a Freddie Mac-backed loan that would normally need 5 percent down, you would be surprised to find your financing had changed. Instead of $12,500 down, you would now need to have $25,000 up front, just to get financing on the home.

Mortgage companies have taken a huge hit over the last few years, and one way they are trying to protect their investments is by making the homebuyer take on more of the risk. Essentially, any market that is deemed a declining one by Freddie Mac and Fannie Mae would have been in danger of a down turn. The two big companies changed their policy on declining markets in 2008, spreading the risk throughout all their products rather than penalizing one particular area of the country, but the criteria they used still work for your own analysis.

If you are looking for a road map to a downturn in the market, here are a few simple signs that the area is headed for trouble:

- Job losses
- New construction stoppages
- Stores going out of business
- An overabundance of "For Sale" signs

Just as you are going to be on the lookout for emerging markets, their flipside will be the market that is still facing a downturn. Obvious markets come to mind, such as the depressed area of Detroit, Michigan where nearly all the jobs have been lost with the hits to the auto industry. That housing market is feeling the sting of mass layoffs and the foreclosures that followed. Other areas with high unemployment will see the same kind of downturn in the near future as residents leave to look for work elsewhere.

If you are looking in an area where there are new construction developments that seem to be frozen in time, you are probably facing a downturn in the market. At one time, new home construction across the country could barely keep up with the demand; now, the opposite is true. With mortgage requirements getting tougher, even people with good credit are finding it nearly impossible to buy homes. The builders, too, are falling on tough times because their financing is dependent on finding buyers for the homes they are building. As buyers become scarce, they find themselves strapped to make the payments on their spec loans.

Homes are not the only things vacant in a market that is experiencing a downturn. Retailers will not hesitate to pull out of areas where they are not making a profit, too. Half-empty shopping centers or commercial construction projects left unfinished are other signs of a market on its way down, rather than up. Just as we mentioned that the big box stores do their homework and move into markets that show promise, they will just as quickly pull out of the ones that do not. You can use their marketing knowledge to help determine where to put your own money.

Finally, an abundance of homes for sale is not a good sign for the market in general. With many houses available for sale and to rent, the likelihood that you will be able to make a successful investment in that area is slim. While real estate investing is long-term, you will want to do your homework and find markets that show some promise and steer clear of the ones that still have further to fall. Of course, it is hard to say what will make a declining market turn into an emerging one or when it will happen. If you already own property in a market that is still falling, it might be worthwhile to hold onto it if you can. If history has taught anything about real estate, it is that it is always changing and will retain value over the long run.

Know when it is time to sell

Recognizing a seller's market is a crucial component to your future success as an emerging markets expert. Ask any savvy investor and they will tell you the days of the seller's market are over — at least for now. The amazing thing about real estate investing — and one of the reasons real estate is such a good long-term investment — is that the market is always changing.

If you have been a buyer of your own home or an investment property, you know who has the upper hand. Maybe you bought your home at the height of the real estate boom of the late nineties/early 21st century, and you had to enter into a bidding war just to stake your claim on a little piece of the American Dream. Or maybe you were forced to buy a property without an inspection because the seller had several offers on the table at once and that was the deciding factor for them. Your offer was the best because it actually required the least from the seller. These circumstances are the essence of the seller's market.

Essentially, a seller's market exists in an area where there are more prospective buyers than there are properties to purchase. The converse of the seller's market, of course, is what many areas are experiencing in 2010 — the glut of homes on the market and the tough mortgage standards is making of a classic buyers market. It is all about supply and demand, and you as a real estate investor want to be on the right side of those scales.

It used to be that finding a seller's market was simple. Everything was basically a seller's market, and homes in foreclosure or distressed properties were hard to come by. These days, houses are in great supply. It seems like a great time to jump in and snatch up foreclosed and distressed properties, but keeping focused on what makes a seller's market can make the difference between success and failure for your real estate investment.

Not all foreclosures are created equal

In a typical American town in 2010, there are hundreds of homes in foreclosure and millions across the country, so why not pick a spot with the lowest-priced homes and buy them? If you are looking to the future and the increase on your investment, you need to consider the economic culture of the market.

There are some places that will always see resurgence: New York City, for instance. In Manhattan alone, there are more than a 1.5 million people, and they all need somewhere to live. While every city has experienced the effects of the recession, a major city like New York has the economic base to support growth whenever it begins to happen. Recognizing that same resilience in smaller communities where properties are available is a little trickier, but it can and should be done.

Economic forecasting for the real estate investor

You might be thinking that it is nearly impossible to determine what markets will emerge from this housing crunch, crisis, or whatever it is being called this month, but you can make some educated estimations based on what kind of information you do have. If you are looking right in your own community or across the country for the kind of market that will pan out to be ripe for investment, the first indicators are employment and industry.

Over the last few decades, our society has moved away from its industrial roots into new areas, like technology. The steel mills have closed and the factory jobs have been moved overseas; new types of business are filling the void in their places. If the area where you want to invest has recently seen a dramatic loss in jobs (which would have also caused an equally dramatic rise in foreclosures), you should tread carefully to make sure that jobs come back. Without available jobs, you will not have potential renters or prospective buyers for your investment property and will likely end up with an extra mortgage every month until you find someone to take it off your hands. Areas where jobs are holding steady are a good pick, as well as areas where jobs are being created. Economists are predicting that job losses will slow throughout the next few years, but in order for the economy to grow, new jobs are necessary. You do not have to be an economist or a financial analyst to do some detective work about the town or community in which you would like to invest. Ask yourself some important questions about the area:

- What draws people to this area?

- How do most people here make a living?

- What does the local economy look like right now, compared to five years ago?

- How much inflation did homes in this area see over the course of the housing "bubble?"

- Are stores moving in or out?

These questions are a great starting point for determining the economic stability of a particular area. For instance, the recession and the loss of jobs have affected the so-called "second home" market. People who were able to maintain a vacation home may have lost their jobs or faced bankruptcy or foreclosure and are losing their vacation property as well as their primary residence. If the distressed property you are buying is in a tourist area, especially a beach or lake town, that is an asset that is not dependent on the local economy so much as the economy as a whole. Purchasing a home in a destination town is usually a sound investment because of the intrinsic value of waterfront property.

Assessing the local economy is also a great way to determine if you have found an emerging seller's market. If the property is located in a small town with only one source of employment, it may be a risky investment. If, instead, it is centrally located between several other larger areas that offer different types of employment, it will be more stable and more likely to weather difficult economic times. Comparing the local current economy to its state just a few years ago will give you an idea of the general direction of the community. Many of the areas that have seen the greatest job losses saw them across the board and happening very quickly. If 75 percent of the jobs in the area were lost within a year, it will take a herculean effort to bring jobs and stability back to that community. If the job loss was more like a slow leak than a burst, the future will probably progress in the same manner.

Just as job loss can be a telling factor, so can the jump (and eventually plunge) in housing prices. In markets that saw increases of more than 200 percent in the matter of just a couple of years, it will take a long time to get back to pre-bubble prices, if that ever happens. If you are looking for an investment property in an area where home prices have deflated less than 25 percent and the home you are purchasing is well below that, it could be a great find. Even seasoned economists cannot be sure what is coming next — everything at this point is conjecture, but purchasing a home in a market that has essentially crashed can be very risky. Finding markets that were less hard-hit may be the key to lucrative real estate investing in the long term.

You may not consider a new McDonald's or Lowe's to be indicators of a seller's market, but they could very well be. Businesses have to stay where they can be supported and are quick to cut and run when their livelihood dries up. If there is significant growth, and buildings and new stores move into the community you are considering, you have the agreement of their business that this may be an emerging seller's market.

One Last Tip: Avoid These Dangerous Mistakes

Real estate has proven to be one of the best, most stable long-term investments you can make. Time and time again, the housing market goes up and down: Supply outweighs demand, and demand outweighs supply. Homes do appreciate in value, and if you are willing to do your homework before the purchase and do the "housework" afterward, it can be rewarding both financially and personally. Investment properties become more than just a number on a spreadsheet; they are real and tangible. They can also help you build personal wealth and, in many cases, bring the satisfaction of helping other people and the communities they live in. The path to successful real estate investing can be bumpy, and if you are not prepared, it could be disastrous. Take a look at some of the common mistakes new investors make when they are jumping in to the investing game.

Thinking it is as easy as it looks on TV

Over the last five to 10 years, cable networks have flooded viewers with shows about real estate investing. These "flippers" buy properties low, quickly make changes to them, and turn around and sell them at a huge profit. It looks easy — after all, how hard can it be to paint a few rooms and refinish the floors? What these shows often do not tell viewers is that the process is much more difficult, and the houses often sit empty after the flippers have poured thousands of dollars into them.

In this market flush with foreclosed and distressed properties, it is tempting to just swoop in and pick up a few properties on the cheap and figure out what to do with them after, but that would be a mistake. Knowing what is involved in investing is the first step to a successful experience, as you are learning from reading this book. It is not as simple as buy, paint, sell, but it can be done and done well if you understand the process and learn all you can about the property, community, and the work that needs to be done before you sign a contract on your first investment property.

What looks like a lot of fun on TV can quickly turn into a financial nightmare if you have not done all the groundwork for your investment property. If you do not personally have the skills to complete the renovation, find someone who can before you make the purchase.

Getting too attached to a property

Many people get into the real estate investing game because they love the thrill of the idea that they could make more money in one transaction than they would in a year at their jobs. Often, the love of houses and the desire to renovate comes in a close second to the desire to make money. When design ideas and producing profits intersect, it can cause real trouble for the new or seasoned investor.

If your love of houses is drawing you into the real estate investing game, be careful to keep those feelings in check when it comes to selecting properties. Finding a beautiful old Victorian or a mid-century modern and restoring it to its former beauty may be fulfilling and rewarding, but it may not pay off big or at all in the long run. Letting your emotions take over what should be a business transaction is always a mistake, whether you are purchasing your own home for your family to live in, or you are selecting a good investment property. Even that perfect house with all the potential will not make you any money if the neighborhood will not support the kind of renovation you have in mind.

You do not want to live in the most expensive house on the block, and you do not want to try to sell the most expensive, either. You need to tailor your purchases and the improvements you make to the budget you have to work with and to the comparable homes in the neighborhood. Many investors fall prey to getting too attached to their properties and want to see them restored or renovated beyond what the market will bear, ending up losing tens of thousands of dollars in the process. Be smart and keep your heart out of the process.

Losing sight of the long-term goals

Flipping houses and real estate investing have been around forever. Owning land, property, and homes was one of the first ways that people were able to build wealth, and that has not changed today. Even with the craziness of the past few years, real estate is still a solid investment when you know what you are getting into. What used to be a buy low, sell high market where homes could be scooped up, painted, primped, and sold for a huge profit in a matter of a few weeks or months has become a longer-term market. The days of quick sales and even quicker re-sales have been replaced with the return of the long-term investment, which is not a bad thing, even for a new investor.

Buying a property has to mean knowing your "exit plan," as savvy investors call it. Basically, it involves having several plans for the property in question because with market fluctuations and the continued job loss that has been plaguing the nation, it may be hard to make certain that your original plan will pan out. Say you purchase a duplex with the intention of fixing up both sides and then selling them individually. If the local area does not have buyers, or the interested buyers are not able to come up with financing, you will need a backup plan.

One way investors have made this mortgage problem into an opportunity is with the lease purchase option. It benefits both the prospective buyer, who can move into what will essentially be their property, and the seller, who can cover expenses and possibly make a tidy profit while the buyer's down payment accrues interest. This option keeps your assets covered and helps you avoid the undesirable circumstance of having to pay a mortgage on an empty property. Lease purchases are not the only ways to look, but they are good ways.

Skipping your homework

Real estate investing can be fast-paced and exciting, and it is the easiest thing in the world to get swept up in that excitement and purchase a property without first doing your homework. From inspections to financing to checking out the local market, there is a lot to be done before you can get started on your investing career. Skipping crucial steps will only hurt you in the long run, so do not worry that taking an extra day or week to check out the neighborhood or double-check your finances will stop you from getting that perfect property. As mentioned earlier, there is no perfect property; there are only solid investments.

Researching the neighborhood and local economy will pay off each and every time you do it. You will know what comparable homes have sold for in the area, as well as what types of renters might be interested in your property once you have it in the condition to rent it out. Doing your homework also means getting to know your financing forward and backward because the last thing you want is a huge surprise at closing. Rushing the process will not help you — a mistake or oversight in the financing could mean that the whole deal will fall apart before you can close on the property, or you may end up facing even worse surprises when the terms of the loan change. It is tempting when you feel like you are up against the clock to skip over important items, such as inspections, but when you are a new investor, it is essential to have all your bases covered, or you may find that you are in way over your head down the road.

Overestimating your abilities, while underestimating the work

Impatience is common among rookie investors, and many of the mistakes discussed are due to getting caught up in all the excitement of finding and buying a property. This mistake and the next are due more to arrogance than impatience. Do not be offended — it takes a large dose of confidence to be able to be a successful real estate investor, but sometimes even the most experienced investors bite off more than they can chew.

With a large profit in mind, new investors often overestimate how much work they can do on the properties they are purchasing. Unless you are a licensed contractor, plumber, electrician, or carpenter, you will likely need professional help with any property you are going to re-sell or rent out. When you are just getting started in the investment game, you may not have a lot of working capital so it stands to reason that doing the work yourself would save you a great deal of money. This, however, can be a huge mistake. Even if you have done home improvement work, the renovations on an investment property can be overwhelming and problems can crop up, making even a small project into a huge undertaking.

Repairs to a property that will be sold or rented are subject to local building codes, and a buyer will inspect the property if you intend to sell it. Overestimating your ability to make repairs can put you behind schedule and cause you to over-budget when it comes time to get the house making money for you. The last thing you want to do is end up having to hire someone to re-do the work you have tried to do yourself.

Going it alone

Real estate investing offers great potential for generating income, and it can be tempting to go it alone to try to save money and increase your profits. But, knowing when to get help is essential for long-term success. Using a Realtor for the purchase can help you navigate the offer process and will ensure that all steps are taken in the right way to complete the transaction. Going under the radar and trying to purchase a property without a Realtor or legal representation can backfire when it comes time for the closing.

Once you have made the purchase, hiring a property manage to take care of rental properties can take the burden of every-day issues off the investor. This will leave your time and energy free to research and develop more properties that will generate much more income than you need to spend on the property manager's salary. Likewise, it is good to know when you need to bring in help with the property. As discussed in the last section, understanding your limitations is key to getting a home into good enough condition to be rented or sold. If you think about your investment of time and money, it is worth it to get the right professional help when necessary.

Misreading a market

Wishful thinking has led many investors down the wrong path. Liking a property too much, but not reading the signals that the area or the market is headed downward is a sure path to losing money on your investment. It can be tempting to jump on a distressed or foreclosure property because the price is so cheap — and in this climate, prices can be cheaper than we could have imagined just a few years ago. If you do not take the market into consideration, however, your cheap house could turn into a very expensive nightmare.

Sometimes, emotions and greed get in the way of making a calm and rational decision about which properties will be sound, long-term investments and which are just cheap and enticing. This book explores what the emerging markets of this new economy look like and how to find them even amongst all the seemingly great deals that are out there now. Understanding what makes a market healthy or unhealthy, promising or declining will serve you well as you begin to identify properties for your investment portfolio.

Getting greedy

Sometimes it is hard to know when to cut your losses and let go, but it can mean the difference between breaking even and losing your shirt when it comes to real estate. In this new market economy, the mantra might be "buy lower, sell low," as opposed to the "buy low, sell high" of a few years ago. Just as you are able to easily find distressed and low-cost properties, other investors and buyers are able to, as well. Knowing the limitations of the property you are buying will help you keep profit in perspective and help you price your property correctly so you will actually make a profit. Getting a solid price for a property, even if it is much lower than you had hoped, is always better than holding onto a property hoping to get a windfall that will never happen.

Holding onto a property with the intention of getting an unrealistic price for it can have devastating consequences. Although you may feel the property is worth $150,000, the comparable properties might be selling for $85,000. Your beautifully renovated home may seem worth a lot more, but in reality it is only worth what the market will bear. Keeping it priced higher when the market does not support it will only lose you money in the long run, whether it is the sale price or the monthly rent. Bringing your expectations down to reality can mean the difference between a profit and a loss. Do not let greed get in the way.

Putting all your eggs in one basket

As a new investor, you may have found your dream property, but the truth of the matter is that successful real estate investing over time is based on much more than one successful flip or rental property. It is a game of numbers and the more properties you own, the greater your wealth will be. One of the best things about real estate investing is that the more property you own, the easier it is to obtain more. Your properties can act as collateral for getting financing and can serve to prove your worthiness as an investor.

It is essential, therefore, to have a long-term strategy when you start investing in real estate so that you are not tied to one home or one deal for the long run. Always having a property in hand, one being rented, and more being explored for the next investment is the best way to ensure success. If one property fails, you will have other investments to cushion the blow. Likewise, if several properties are generating income for you, those will give you both the leeway and the leverage to make more risky, and possibly more lucrative, investments. Because real estate is true ownership, it will always retain some value. Just as you would develop a varied and large stock portfolio, so should you keep your mind on the idea of a property portfolio.

Misunderstanding the financing

Financing after the housing bubble burst and the mortgage crisis is a whole new world. The days of easy and loose finance terms, and even easier refinancing, are long gone. What has replaced them is the tightening of loan terms and harder-to-meet criteria for borrowers. This will affect you both as a buyer of investment properties and as a seller of those same properties.

Understanding your loan has always been important in buying a property, and now more than ever you must know the terms of your loans inside and out before signing any paperwork. Adjustable rate loans, interest only loans, and jumbo mortgages still exist, but the climate of increasing home prices does not. This combination of circumstances means that investors need to be even more careful about their loan terms.

While it is easy to make mistakes when you are starting out in real estate investing, the best advice for anyone is to be prepared. Researching and having a good understanding of the financing and condition of properties will be your best defense against the common problems people face when getting started. Using the examples of seasoned investors and keeping everything as a business transaction will ensure your success as you become an investor.

CASE STUDY: RENTING YOUR INVESTMENTS DURING HOLDING

John and Chris Macdonald, rental specialists

Owning a rental property may seem like an easy way to make money in this volatile housing market, but there are many factors to take into consideration before taking the plunge into being a landlord.

The Macdonalds have been landlords for more than five years, renting nine apartment properties to students, each with 28–33 tenants at a time. With three children a busy schedule, owning rental properties has been a worthwhile source of income for this family.

The biggest challenge they face with renting mainly to college students is collecting timely rental payments and dealing with potential damage to the property. There is also a high turnover in this type of rental situation that would not exist if the properties were rented to families. Having a property manager who lives close to the apartments is essential to the success of their properties because he is able to handle the day-to-day problems that crop up with tenants, especially in their case where they are more than an hour away from their complex.

When the Macdonalds decided to expand their property holdings, they wanted to take advantage of the declining real estate market and buy distressed properties in neighborhoods that were still show-ing promise. They considered the proximity to parks and schools, as well as the overall condition of the neighborhoods and the amount of homeownership in the area. After employing contractors to make the necessary repairs to the homes, they rent them out to families. They also are working to put lease/purchase contracts into place with tenants so they will eventually assume ownership of the property. As with their college rentals, the couple employs property managers for these homes. In this case, the property manager is responsible for collecting rent, and takes his commission from the payment. He also handles repairs or other problems that come up, drawing funds from an account they have set up to handle such situations.

They caution that some properties may be vacant for a time before a tenant can be found, but the opportunity to make money in real estate rentals is still very real. The possibility of having an empty rental property is one of the challenges with this type of rental, and can be tough for the new investor. Keeping the long-term in mind with regards to buying rental properties is important, whatever type of property you choose.

Their best advice to new investors would be to hire a property man-ager to handle the daily needs of the rentals, like collecting rent and making minor repairs. Of course, having a property manager is an additional expense, but it is one that the Macdonalds would recom-mend to anyone considering becoming a landlord. Unless you are planning to make managing your rental properties a full-time job, having a property manager is the best way to handle the rentals and the inevitable problems that arise.

Chapter 12
Making the Big Sale

Real estate investing can be exhilarating, infuriating, confusing, frustrating, and, best of all, profitable. When you purchase a property, you ultimately have the goal of selling it at a profit in mind, whether that will be in six months or six years. Getting your property sold poses its own special challenges. As with all the steps of investing in real estate, the more you know and the more prepared you are, the better your experience will be. Putting in the work ahead of time will reward you with a bigger payday.

How To Determine a Property's Real Value

The sale of your property, and ultimately the amount of profit you make on the venture, will begin with determining the value. Price and value are not exactly the same when it comes time to sell a home. The price will be whatever the market will bear. The value to the seller is what you owe, plus what you have spent renovating the property, plus, of course, your profit margin.

Talking with a real estate agent about comparable homes in the neighborhood will give you a clearer idea of when to sell a property. If the value of the home is in line with the prices in the area, you are set to make a good profit on the home. If the value is much lower than the going price for comparable homes, you would be wise to hold onto the property until the market rebounds in the area and you can recoup your investment and make a profit with a sale.

Take new construction as an example of value versus price. Savvy investors have scooped up new construction properties where the buyer was unable to finalize his or her financing and the builder had to sacrifice the home at a loss. In that case, you may have gotten a new home for about $50,000 less than what the builder was charging the original buyer, paying only $300,000 for a $350,000 home. The builder has now finalized the development and only re-sales are available. But, the market may have cooled since that purchase and homes in the neighborhood are now selling for $325,000. The home you purchased still has a good enough value to consider selling it. With very little investment on your part, since the house was new did not need renovation, you are able to turn a profit of $25,000 in a sluggish market.

Once you have determined the real value of your property, you will need to set a price, which can be tricky business.

Pricing practices

If you are already working with a real estate broker, this process can be easier if you can rely on their expertise in setting an asking price. It can be difficult to find the right starting point — one that is not so high as to scare away buyers and not too low as to make a buyer think twice that there may be something wrong with the property. Finding that perfect middle ground is essential to selling a house quickly and for the best profit. Even in a buyer's market, effective pricing can generate multiple offers, which translate into more profit for you as the seller. You might think that there is not money to be made in a buyer's market, but with the right tools and knowledge, smart real estate investors are making a profit when selling their properties.

One thing to keep in mind is that most buyers are using the Internet as their first stop in looking for a home. Few people are calling agents first anymore; instead, they are checking out Web sites where they can tour hundreds of homes before they ever set foot in one of them. In order to get that Internet buyer, you will want to price your property within the popular search parameters. Most real estate Web sites lump homes into price categories based on either $100,000 increments or $50,000 increments as the price goes higher. Listing your home for $351,500 will immediately eliminate all those prospective buyers who have capped their searches at $349,900. It may seem like an insignificant detail, but the right price point opens the door to the right buyer.

The most important reason you want to get the price right the first time is to sell the house as quickly as possible without having to lower the asking price during the process. If you start out way too high, you may get a number of lowball offers, which may only strengthen your resolve to stick it out with the price you have. The unfortunate part about holding out is the dreaded days on market (DOM) in the Multiple Listing Service (MLS). DOM is a great indicator for prospective buyers. If your DOM goes above 21 days, you can expect either low offers or few offers to come in. You have priced yourself out of the market.

By determining and setting a reasonable or modest asking price, you are setting yourself up for multiple offers. People know that it is a buyer's market, and they are looking for good deals. But, if your house has the whole package-price, quality, and the right look, you can expect that you will get a good price in the end.

Making Sense of the Comps

In the language of real estate agents, comps are everything when it comes to setting price, but what does that really mean? Comparable listings are by far the biggest standard that people use to set a fair listing price for a property. Here are some of the factors that go into finding the right comps for your property:

- Square footage
- Location
- Age of the home
- Style of home
- Home condition
- Outdoor space

Looking at recently sold, active listings and even pending sales can give you the best picture of the value of your property and the price you should set for selling.

A Word About Brokers

Real estate agents can make or break the sale of your property. A good agent is worth his or her weight in gold because he or she will possess skills and experience that you might not have. Finding that perfect agent can be tough, but it is worth doing the research to find a successful and dynamic agent who understands the current market, uses all the marketing tools available, and is ready to sell your home. Here are few tips to aid in your search:

- **Look for online presence:** You want a real estate agent who is using every type of technology he or she can to market your home.

- **Quick response time:** Even a busy agent knows he or she has to get back to you quickly. If more than a day goes by without a return call, move on to the next prospect.

- **Sold properties:** Results speak volumes, so check out their portfolio of homes for variety, prices, and sold prices compared with asking prices to see what kind of performance record they have.

- **A good fit:** Working with an agent can often be emotional and tiring, so finding one who is a good fit personality- and temperament-wise is a good idea. If your Realtor speaks so slowly that it drives you crazy, you will not have a good working relationship.

- **Experience:** This market calls for a certain level of expertise, so do not give the job to your cousin who just got his real estate license. You want to choose someone who knows what investors needs are and how to meet them.

Once you have made your choice and enlisted the help of a broker, you will find that he or she will generally take care of the rest of the matters in this section. The broker's expertise and assistance can be invaluable throughout the process, and if you are a busy investor, meaning that you have other projects in the works, your reliance on a Realtor may be just what you need to keep your concentration elsewhere. Developing a good relationship with a broker early in your investing career can pay off in huge dividends down the line when that same broker can keep you informed about investment opportunities.

An experienced agent has the experience to help you through the marketing, listing, and selling of your home, and can also ensure that your closing goes smoothly because they have the necessary contacts for all facets of closing the sale. Although many investors have the can-do attitude that they can handle it all on their own, knowing when to seek help is just as important as that adventurous spirit. As with enlisting other types of help, such as property managers and contractors, having a agent in your corner leaves you free to pursue other investments and manage your other properties — all while building wealth and your portfolio of real estate investments.

Establish a Solid Marketing Plan

You might not automatically think of selling a property as tied to a marketing plan, but you should. Just as retailers set up a marketing plan for new products, so will you or your agent must devise a multi-faceted strategy for selling your property. With so many avenues for advertising a home, it is important to break the process down into steps and take each one individually. Ideally, your hard work on the marketing plan will pay off with your home spending just a short time on the market, generating multiple offers and providing you with a nice profit when all is said and done. The basics for a marketing plan to sell your investment property include:

Preparing for the sale: Making sure the house is in move-in condition and that all repairs and improvements are done prior to showing the property are essential to a quick sale. If there is no grass in the front yard, delay putting the property on the market until it is done because you only get one chance to make a good first impression with a buyer, especially in today's competitive market.

Listing the property for maximum exposure: If you are using a Realtor, he or she will likely use the ubiquitous MLS for your property. It is basically a searchable database that is available to all Realtors and Web sites so that your home will be at the fingertips of other agents and prospective buyers.

Use multi-media advertising: The Internet is huge, and it is the main advertising source for real estate and most other products we buy or sell. Of course, your property should be well represented with Web site access. This also means taking many well-lit, flattering photos of the home and posting them on the Web site. The more enticing you can make your listing, the more traffic you will create to your property. Even with the popularity of Internet marketing, other avenues, such as real estate books, newspaper ads, and television spots should be used to generate buzz about your property.

Curb appeal: One of the most popular, low-tech ways to generate interest in your property is a box of flyers on the sign at the actual property. Many prospective buyers are first intrigued by a "For Sale" sign at the home and will stop to pick up a flyer, then visit the Web site or call the agent (or you, if you are selling the home directly).

Networking: Either you or your Realtor should constantly be talking up your property and using personal and business contacts to get the word out about the listing. Your Realtor can work with other agents to try to find the right buyer for your property.

Open houses: The old-fashioned open house often draws more curious neighbors than it does prospective buyers, but they can be effective and can draw out multiple offers if more than one person attending the open house shows an interest. Anything that creates a sense of urgency in the buyer is a good thing, and open houses often serve that purpose well.

Whether you are creating your own marketing plan or relying on the aid of a real estate broker, marketing the home correctly and effectively is the best way to get it sold quickly and for a good profit. The longer the home sits on the market, the more money you will be spending on mortgage payments and insurance. An empty house does not make the investor any money.

Getting the Word Out

Advertising your home in this tough market is even more important than ever. Some of the best ways to reach prospective buyers are:

- Internet marketing
- Newspaper ads
- Television spots
- Flyers
- Open houses
- Broker open houses
- Signage at the property
- Flyers available at property
- Neighborhood marketing

Being creative and aggressive in marketing your home could make the difference and get it sold faster.

Determine Your Sales Methods

There are several ways to sell homes, and you should consider the benefits of each before deciding which is right for you. As mentioned earlier, you can contract a real estate broker, which is the most common way of selling property, or you can sell it yourself through traditional means or through an auction. Each method has its own benefits and drawbacks, so understanding them is important in making that decision.

Multiple listings

If you have enlisted the help of a Realtor, he or she will put your home into the MLS. This searchable database puts your home at the fingertips of buyers and other agents. In a Realtor-brokered sale, there are usually two agents at work. The buyer's agent, depending on state laws, generally only works for the buyer and has their interests first and foremost in their concern. The seller's agent works for you and is your advocate during the process. Each agent works within the legal parameters to get the best price for their client. In some cases, and under certain conditions, a Realtor may serve as a buyer's and seller's agent in the same transaction, but that is rare.

Once your home is listed in the MLS, the Realtor will begin actively marketing the property. A good Realtor will put the previously discussed types of marketing into action and use all their personal and professional contacts to get the property sold. Remember that although you pay a commission to the Realtor at closing, they do not get paid unless your home gets sold. The broker takes on all the expense and work of developing and implementing the marketing plan, and looks forward to the payday when the home gets sold.

Choosing a Realtor and the MLS is good for the hands-off investor who wants to find someone they trust and leave the selling of the property in their hands. As discussed before, if your main objective is finding and developing new investment properties, you should delegate as much of the other work as possible. Relying on an experienced professional to do the leg-work of selling your home can be a smart decision. Developing a professional relationship with a great Realtor can only help you as an investor.

Direct sell or for sale by owner (FSBO)

Many investors like to keep everything under their thumb, and this type of selling is appealing because you are in control of every aspect of the sale. If you have the interest and skills to sell your own property, you stand to save both your own Realtor's commission fees and the commission fees of the buyer's agent at the closing on the property. In a tight market, those fees can take a sizable chunk out of your profit, especially if your profit margins are low. When the buy-low, sell-high days were here, a 6 percent commission was nothing. In these days of smaller profits, however, that small amount can make a big difference for your bottom line as an investor.

So, the biggest advantage to selling your own property is that you will avoid paying out a commission to someone else. The pitfalls are that you may not have the experience and know-how to get the house sold in a reasonable amount of time. Realtors that understand the market can be invaluable at getting the house priced right, and this is where many investors change their minds about hiring a Realtor. They decide to choose their own price and list the home themselves. If you choose to sell your property yourself, keep in mind that you will have to create a marketing plan, take the time to show the property to interested buyers and follow up with all the details of closing. When you consider all the work that goes into the big sale, the commission fees of a Realtor may not seem so significant.

Selling at auction

You might have the image of a suited auctioneer standing on the steps of a foreclosed property, yelling "SOLD!" to the highest bidder, while the displaced homeowner slinks off in shame. That image is not today's auction, however, and auctions are not just for distressed properties anymore. Auctions give investors what selling a home on the real estate market cannot — a deadline. An auction is a fixed date when you know you will have a buyer for your home, if you can market the home and the auction well enough to generate interest.

Hiring a professional auction company is nearly essential to the success of auctioning off a home. A reputable company will know the regulations inside and out, and have a procedure in place for making sure that buyers are pre-qualified to weed out ineligible bidders. Just as you could benefit from the marketing plan of a Realtor, most auctioneers will have a plan to get your home sold at auction. After all, they only get paid their fees when your home sells.

There are two basic types of real estate auctions:

- **Reserve auction:** You will set a reserve, or minimum price, below which the house will not sell. Unless your interested buyers bid up to that price, the house will remain unsold, and you will likely owe a fee to the auction company for their work and time.

- **Absolute auction:** The house will sell at whatever the highest bid of the day is. In bank absolute auctions, a lucky seller will oftentimes walk away paying only back taxes or property liens. With an auction on a quality, renovated home, an absolute auction may generate a bidding war. The thought that buyers might get a great deal will draw more buyers.

Your auction company can advise you of your local market and what you can expect from each type of auction in your area. The biggest benefit of an auction for you as an investor is that end date; you will know when the house will sell, and you will not be incurring anymore carrying costs. Whichever method you decide is best for selling your property, you should still become as familiar as possible with the process because it is vital for the success of your first big sale and all sales that will follow.

Analyzing Letters of Intent

You may have written a letter of intent (LOI), but your first sale may be the first time you are on the receiving end of such correspondence. Therefore, you will need to understand both what is contained in the letter and what is implied. Simply stated, a letter of intent precedes a formal contract and contains the buyer's intent to purchase a property, including the conditions under which the sale may take place. Typically, it will include all of the following:

- Buyer and seller information

- Descriptive information about the property in question

- The actual offer or intent of the prospective buyer, which includes:

  o Offered purchase price

  o Financing and down payment information

  o Terms or conditions, including the request for a home inspection

  o Contingency information

  o Closing date

  o Due diligence time for having a clear title and filing forms

- Non-binding language portion

- Signature of buyer and space for the seller's signature

For the seller, the most important portions of the LOI are the ones that pertain to the finances and the timeline. Obviously, you will need to analyze the offer letter because your best tools as a seller will be comparing offers and making counter-offers to buyers you feel are serious and the best qualified to make a move on the property. You will naturally be drawn first to the offer price on the property, but not all offers are created equal. In the next section, how to handle multiple offers will be discussed, but for now, assess what information a single letter of intent contains.

The purchase price is important, but the price on the letter of intent can be a starting point. In this market, many people have the idea that they can purchase something for nothing. Even after you have taken the time to price your home just right for the local market and quality of the property, you may get some lowball offers. Do not take it personally. Just as you are hoping to get the most for the property, the buyer is trying to pay the least. You can always prepare a counter-offer, which will give the prospective buyers a wake-up call and let them see what price you are comfortable with. In a buyer's market, you can expect a little negotiation.

The best buyers, meaning the most serious and most able to complete the purchase, will have financing secured already and will not have a property to sell themselves. If a buyer has a property to sell, he or she will disclose that with a contingency clause, stating that they have to first sell their current home to make the purchase of your property. The timeline is equally important to you as the investor: A quick sale is always best in any market and even more important in this market. The sooner you can go to closing the better.

When both parties, seller and buyer, have agreed upon and signed the letter of intent, a formal contract will be written. This is where the Realtors get really involved and where you will need representation if you are selling your home yourself. The legal proceedings and paperwork involved in real estate transactions are not for amateurs, and one missed form can mean problems down the line.

The closing on a property generally involves several parties: the buyer, seller, legal representation for each party, a mortgage representative, and a title insurer. Each person has his or her individual role to fill, and this is where choosing the right real estate agent will pay off. Assembling the right team to make the closing a smooth process is the most important part of the whole procedure. The best way to get through closing is to have representation, either in the form of your agent or a real estate attorney. Having a professional person whose sole responsibility is to protect your interests will be invaluable. With more complicated transactions, such as those involving multiple investors or several escrow accounts, a real estate attorney can be a great help, even if you already have the assistance of an agent.

Juggling Multiple Offers

Imagine that you have renovated your first property and have contracted a Realtor to put it up for sale. You have taken the time to make the home look its best and your Realtor has pulled out all the stops with his or her fantastic marketing plan. Now, after just three weeks on the market, you have received three offers on a 4-bedroom home with half an acre of land, a pool, and a great school district. You originally wanted to list the home for $400,000, but your Realtor helped you adjust that price for the market and you settled on $375,000. Now, look at the three offers and how they compare to each other:

	Offer No. 1	Offer No. 2	Offer No. 3
Offer price	$355,000	$350,000	$360,000
Financing	Standard mortgage 20 percent down, pre-approved	Working out details to borrow from relatives	Pre-approved, no money down
Terms and conditions	Contingent on inspection and sale of current home	Will take the property as-is, no inspection or contingency on sale	Contingent on inspection, seller to pay closing costs
Closing date	120 days	45 days	60 days

By using the information in this table, you can easily compare the offers on the property. They all have one thing in common — none of them are close to your asking price. That may come as a shock at first, but on closer inspection, there is more information there. The first offer is promising because of their financing, but their closing date would be the farthest away. The second offer sounds a little fishy and without financing in order, it would be unwise to pursue this one and give a counter-offer. The third offer is the highest, but with no money to put down on the property, they may find that their financing has disappeared before they are able to close, since many banks have reduced or eliminated their 100 percent financing options.

Faced with these offers, a smart investor would work them to his or her advantage. If you are using a Realtor, your agent will be able to communicate with the buyer's agents that there are multiple offers. Now, the ball is in the buyer's court and they have to come back with their best offer. The negotiation has begun.

Negotiating the best possible offer

Using the same offers from the last section, suppose you create a counter-offer for each of the two qualified buyers. Your counter could be something like the following:

- $370,000
- No sale contingency
- 90-day closing
- Inspection contingency accepted
- Seller will pay closing

Now, the waiting game will begin. Your two prospective buyers will come back with their best offers; knowing that there is another interested party always puts the pressure on. You may not get everything you want in the final contract, but you have used your Realtor's knowledgeable pricing and the buzz he or she was able to create about your property to your advantage. You are in the envied position because two people want your property.

Of course, if there is no swaying you from your original asking price, you can hold out and accept nothing less. Only you can make that decision with your Realtor helping you decide what is best. The situation you want to avoid is the one where you have turned down too many offers or, worse yet, other properties in the same neighborhood start selling for much less. Finding the right price is a delicate process, and only the actual sale will truly show what the market will bear.

A Note About Inspections

As the seller, you may think that the inspection is none of your concern, but you can do some pro-active work and have a certified inspector examine your property before putting it up for sale. You can eliminate some of the worry and the wait with a certified inspector report ready for the buyer. Most smart buyers will want to know what they are getting into-your inspection report can save time and headaches at the time of sale.

10 Rules to Succeed in Emerging Markets

Selling your first investment property may be even more exhausting than when you purchased it, but solid information and a plan will get you through it, making you ready for the next sell. In changing real estate markets, it is more essential than ever to do the work you need to do to get your house ready to sell. An empty investment property is like a hole in your pocket — it just makes you lose money. Enlisting the right kind of help at the right time can make all the difference and can keep your profit margin as high as possible in a cool market.

You have learned a lot of common sense tips and tricks in this book to help you become a successful investor. Take a moment now to revisit the top ten rules that you must follow to succeed:

1. Pay Less than a Property is Worth

A property is only an investment if you can make a profit on it. That requires buying property at a discount. Even if you are sure that a certain property is going to gain value in the future, you must buy it at a discount now to reap the biggest reward later.

2. Use Other People's Money as Much as Possible

Finding other people to invest in your dream is a surefire way to success. Only using your own funds limits what you can buy and how long you can hold it. By bringing in other investors, you create new possibilities and expand your horizons.

3. Make Sure the Property is Generating Income

Unless you are independently wealthy and do not care if your investment property loses money, you had better make sure that any property you buy can pay for itself through rentals. Unlike flipping, which requires you buy a house, fix it up, and sell it fast, emerging markets investing takes time. The costs of holding a property this long can become astronomical if you do not have some way of making the property pay for itself in the interim.

4. Use IRS Rules for Your Benefit

The IRS offers quite a few tax advantages to real estate investors. Be sure to learn all you can about these rules and loopholes so you can come out ahead at tax time.

5. Never Use Your IRA Funds to Buy or Hold a Property

New investors often want to use their best source for cash to get into the game: their IRA. This is a terrible idea for several reasons. First, an IRA is a long-term investment that must not be touched in order to grow properly. The fees for early withdrawal can topple up to 40 percent. If that is not enough of an incentive to leave your IRA alone, consider this fact: If you make a mistake, you will not have a retirement fund left. If you cannot find the funds to invest elsewhere, reconsider your plan.

6. Build a Solid Investment Team

Success in the emerging markets field takes a good team of experts to guide you through each phase of the demanding process. No investor, especially one brand new to the game, can be expected to know it all. Those who admit this are the ones who succeed. Those who do not often find themselves broke.

7. Residential Properties are Best for New Investors

It takes a lot of skill and experience to win at commercial real estate. It is best for novice investors to begin with smaller, less expensive, and less risky residential properties, only moving on to bigger investment once they have built their knowledge base and professional network.

8. Buy in Areas You Know Well

The importance of expanding your search for new properties was discussed, but be sure to buy in areas that you personally know well, or have taken a good bit of time to research. Otherwise, you may make a costly mistake: believing an area is emerging when it is not.

9. Pick a Niche

Become an expert in one area of real estate like residential homes, condos, or small apartments, and buy in that niche until you are ready to expand. There is plenty to learn in this business and if you do not take the time to learn the nuances of each niche, you will likely make a costly mistake before too long.

10. Get in and Get Dirty

If there is one business that requires a hands-on approach, it is investing in emerging markets. While it is important to have a reliable team to work with, it is equally important to be willing to get your hands dirty. All successful investors hit the streets looking for their own properties; are not afraid to do some of the hard labor themselves; and can easily make quick decisions regarding the purchase, remodel, and sale of a property. There may come a time when you hire out a good portion of the day-to-day work, but to remain successful you will have to be willing to put on some work gloves from time to time and get dirty.

Conclusion

How Much Money Can I Expect To Make?

If there is one question on the mind of every person reading this book it is, "How much money can I expect to make if I invest in emerging markets?" This is not an easy question to answer, but this book will attempt to give you some idea of what to expect by offering some practical tips that will help determine the amount of profit each of your investment properties will likely generate. Here is a review of some of the basics already covered.

First, a few facts: Emerging markets are higher risk, higher profit yield properties. To be considered an emerging market, a property should generate at least a 20–50 percent profit, and even more in some cases. Plus, emerging markets are just that: emerging. They are not bought for a quick turnaround and are located in up-and-coming areas that have not yet hit their pricing peak; that is what makes them profitable. These are not properties that can or should be quickly flipped. Most emerging markets are held for at least six to 18 months before they are put back on the market, and many are held even longer.

The amount of money you can make on this type of investment depends are several factors:

- When you enter the market
- How much you paid for the property
- How long you are willing to wait to resell it
- The dynamics of the neighborhood
- Pure luck

A good investor with a knack for spotting up-and-coming areas may be able to enter the market so early and hold so long that they can easily double or triple the price they paid on a property when they resell it. It is not uncommon for an experienced emerging markets specialist to buy a property for $100,000 and resell it for $500,000 five or six years later. New investors should not count on profits this large, however. That is a skill that takes perfecting.

Plan on at least doubling your money in order to make an investment worthy of your time, energy, and money when investing in emerging markets. If you do not believe that a $100,000 investment will reap at least $100,000 or more in profits after the sale, you may want to reconsider buying that property. Remember, emerging market investors do not just buy one or two properties; they own dozens. In order to have the cash on hand to hold these properties until the market rebounds, they must be able to make huge profits in the end. This is not about greed; it is about survival.

Estimate your initial costs, ongoing carrying costs, and final sales price to see what kind of profit margin each property will dictate. If the profit is not large enough, find another property in which to invest.

Finally, think about how much money you want to make in emerging real estate. Set a goal and do not let anything stand in your way of achieving it. If you do not think a $35,000 profit is worth your time and trouble, then only buy properties that you feel will generate the kinds of sales prices and profits you want.

When it comes to emerging markets, the sky is the limit. No one can predict what real estate is going to do and which homes will spike in price in the coming years. But, if you think you have what it takes to evaluate each situation and make a reasonable prediction as to its future, jump aboard the emerging markets gravy train. There are billions of dollars to be made in emerging markets in the coming years. Whether or not you are one of the few to reap the profits of others' financial demise is up to you. Do you have the guts to take a risk when everyone else is playing it safe? If so, then you just might walk away a huge winner. The choice is yours.

Glossary

When you talk real estate, it often feels like you are speaking another language — at least for those who are new to the investment game. That is why this basic glossary is included. Use it as a reference as you read through this book and begin your emerging markets career. By no means all-inclusive, it should give you the definitions of the most basic terms you will come across while beginning your new career as a real estate mogul.

Abnormal sale: A house or property sells for more or less than its current market value — for instance, 25 percent less than comparable homes nearby. Appraisers can ignore abnormal sales when comparing similar properties for value.

Abstract of title: The summarized history of a piece of real estate. It describes each time the property changed hands and notes all encumbrances that have lessened its value or use. This document is certified as complete and truthful by the abstractor.

Acceptance: Completion of a sales contract when someone offers to buy a property under specific terms and the owner accepts.

Acquisition appraisal: A government agency determines how much to pay a property owner after acquiring their property via negotiation or condemnation.

Acquisition cost: The total price someone pays for a property, with all fees added in.

Adjustable-rate Mortgage (ARM): Unlike a fixed-rate loan, this home loan has a changing interest rate, which fluctuates to stay current with rates of mortgage loans. It can also change with indexes of the government or financial market.

Adjustment date: On this day, the interest rate changes for an adjustable-rate mortgage.

Adjustment period: For an adjustable-rate mortgage, this is the time period between changes in interest rate.

Adviser: An investment banker or a broker representing a property owner during a real estate transaction. The adviser collects a fee when transaction or financing ends.

Aesthetic value: Worth of a property determined by its beauty.

Affidavit of title: A statement written under oath by a real estate grantor or seller and recognized by a notary public. The person gives his identity, confirms that the title has not changed for the worse since it was last examined, and officially declares that he possesses the property (if appropriate).

Affordability index: A measure designed by the National Association of Realtors to describe how affordable houses are for residents buying in a given area.

Agreement of sale: A legal document giving the terms and price of a property sale, which both parties sign.

Alienation: Property going to a new owner by sale, gift, adverse possession, or eminent domain.

Annual percentage rate (APR): The "real" cost of borrowing money. The APR includes all credit costs, including a loan's interest rate, origination fees, and insurance.

Appraisal report: The report an appraiser writes describing a property's value, summarizing how it was determined.

Appraised value: The monetary value of a property given in an appraisal report.

Appreciation: The process of a home or property gaining value, which can stem from several factors, including additions to the building, changes in financial markets, and inflation.

ARM (adjustable-rate mortgage) index: An openly published number that guides how adjustable-rate mortgages change.

As-is condition: The buyer or renter accepts the property and its flaws just as they are, giving up the right to insist on repairs or renovations.

Asking (advertised) price: The amount a property owner hopes a buyer will pay, which may change with negotiation.

Assessed value: The value a tax assessor determines a home to have — used for computing a tax base.

Assessor: A public official responsible for valuing properties for tax purposes.

Asset management: All aspects of handling real estate assets from when someone first invests in them until they sell them.

Assumable mortgage: A mortgage that allows the next owner to totally acquire the debt of the first owner. This means they take over the mortgage and its leftover payments.

Auction: Selling personal property or land to the highest bidder, which states can do with foreclosed property. Bidders can make public or private offers, in writing or speech.

Balloon mortgage: A mortgage that takes the amount of a loan and amortizes it over a shorter period of time, with a large payoff sum due at the end of the loan period.

Blanket loan: This mortgage covers multiple pieces of real estate, but partially frees each parcel from the mortgage lien when certain fractions of the debt are repaid.

Blighted areas: Part of a city or other area where the buildings are rundown or needing repair.

Book value: A property's worth as determined by its purchase price and upgrades or additions, minus any depreciation. Corporations use it to indicate their properties' values.

Bridge loan: A short-term loan used to bridge a funding gap between the purchase of one property and the sale of another.

Brownfield: A property where people once used hazardous substances, such as a vacant gas station or closed factory.

Brownstone: A row house adjoining other buildings that stands three to five stories tall.

Bulk sale: A buyer purchases an entire group of real estate assets in different locations.

Buy-back agreement: A contract term saying the seller will purchase a property back if certain events happen.

Buyers' market: A situation where buyers can be choosy about real estate and shrewd about pricing, because there are more properties than buyers. That happens when economies slow, when too many buildings are constructed, or when population numbers fall.

Capitalization rate (CAP): A ratio used to determine the profit on a certain investment. It is calculated by dividing the sale price with the net operating expenses to determine a profit percentage.

Capital appreciation: Growth in a property's value once partial sales and capital improvements are accounted for. It differs from a capital gain, which one receives by selling the property.

Certificate of sale: Document one receives when purchasing a building foreclosed for tax reasons. It proves that the buyer paid the necessary taxes for the redemption period and claimed the property title afterward.

Certificate of title: An attorney's official opinion on who owns the title to a property, or other aspects of its status. The attorney makes this statement after scrutinizing public records.

Chain of title: All the times a title has moved from owner to owner, until the present. Attorneys use this history to evaluate the title's status.

Class A: High-quality property that will bring in a lot of rent money.

Class B: Desirable property that falls short of bringing in the highest rent price possible.

Class C: Low-rent property with acceptable living conditions but sparse amenities.

Clear title: Title free from potential problems or hassles, such as legal encumbrances, defects and liens.

Closing costs: The fees associated with the purchase of a piece of property (insurance, title fees, mortgage fees, broker fees).

Commercial mortgage: Money loaned for businesses to buy their properties or buildings.

Commercial property: Slated for businesses, not homes or residential buildings.

Comparable sales (Comps): The sales amounts of recently sold properties in a specific area that is similar to the one it is being compared to.

Conversion: Assigning property a new use or type of owner-ship — changing a large house into an apartment complex, for instance.

Conveyance: The document stating that a title passes to a new owner. Also means transference of titles between parties (closing).

Cost-approach appraisal: Approximating a property's value by adding the land's worth to the cost an appraiser says one would pay to replace the building, minus depreciation. This approach does not use prices of nearby homes to estimate a building's value.

Curb appeal: A property or home's good looks, as noted by viewers on its street.

Debt service: Total money one needs to pay all the principal and interest of a loan for a certain amount of time.

Debt-to-equity: How much unpaid mortgage a property has, compared with its equity. The ratio would be 1:2 if a property had $100,000 of unpaid debt and $50,000 of equity.

Debt-to-income: What percent of monthly income some-one spends repaying a debt. To calculate, divide the monthly money paid toward the debt by that month's gross income.

Deed: This document legally transfers property to a new owner. That buyer gets the deed after negotiating with and paying the seller.

Deed in lieu of foreclosure: Returning one's property to a lender without foreclosure proceedings, to avoid their negative effects and costs.

Deed restrictions: Restrictions given in a deed on how property can be used. They can limit what kind of new structures people can build there, or what activities or objects are allowed on the property.

Delayed exchange: A party trades property for a second piece of real estate, but does not receive it right away. This delay lets that party defer all taxable gains on the first piece of property.

Depreciation: Appraisers use this term to mean lessened value of a property because it grows old, obsolete, or has other defects. For real estate investors, this term means a tax deduction taken while owning income property.

Direct sales comparisons approach (market comparison approach): An appraiser places a value on property by examining the prices on recently purchased estates nearby with similar qualities.

Disclosure: A document listing all the relevant positive and negative information about a piece of real estate.

Due diligence: Actions by someone looking to purchase real estate — checking the property for defects or hazards and verifying that a seller represents it.

Economic life: How many years an improvement will continue giving property value.

Encumbrance: Anything that diminishes a property's worth or makes it less useful or enjoyable. Examples include taxes, mortgages, easements, judgment liens, and rules restricting how the property is used.

Equity: A property's value minus its liabilities, such as unpaid debts.

Fair market value: Price determined by how much a buyer will agree to pay and how little a seller will accept. In a competitive market, properties would sell at certain times for market value.

Flag lot: Skirting a subdivision's rules by dividing property into distinct parcels.

For sale by owner (FSBO): An owner sells property without using a real estate broker. This owner works directly with the buyer or the buyer's real estate agent.

Freestanding building: A structure separate from others, such as a shed by a house.

Functional obsolescence: A state of lowered value when an improvement is badly designed or loses function, such as a sliding window that sticks and will not open.

General (or master) plan: Used by governments to grow communities in an organized way. This long-term program dictates how property will be developed and used.

Gross income multiplier: A number used to estimate a property's value. One multiplies the property's yearly gross income by this figure.

Highest and best use: Most legal and sensible way one can use property or land, to give it peak value in a financially realistic, well-supported way.

Historic structure: A building given special status for tax purposes because it is officially deemed historically important.

Impact fee: Private developers pay this fee to the city for permission to start a project. The money helps the city build infrastructure, such as sewers, for the new development.

Improvement: Any construction that boosts a property's value, including private structures like buildings and fences, as well as public structures like roads and water piping.

In-house sale: A kind of sale made solely by the broker in the listing agreement, with no other brokers involved. This kind of sale includes situations where the broker finds the buyer, or where the buyer approaches someone working for the broker.

Income property: A piece of real estate the owner uses to earn money without residing there.

Indicated value: How much a piece of real estate is worth, depending on its land value and its cost minus depreciation; the net income it makes during yearly operations; and how much similar properties currently sell for.

Indirect costs: Money spent on development for things besides the labor and materials going directly into structures on the lot.

Inside lot: Surrounded on three sides by other lots and fronted by a road, unlike a corner lot with two sides bordering roads.

Inspection report: A document prepared by a licensed inspector that describes the condition of a property.

Inventory: The amount of real estate on the market, not taking into account its quality or availability.

Investment property: A property that is purchased to either lease, rent, or re-sell for a profit.

Key lot: Property desired for its location, which can allow the owner to use adjacent lots to their full potential. Also, a key lot is a property with its front on a secondary street and one side bordering the rear of a corner lot.

Land description: Legal account of what a piece of property is like.

Landlord: A person who leases property to someone else.

Lease option: An agreement giving the tenant a purchasing option for the property for a certain amount of money after a certain amount of time renting.

Lien: A recorded claim against a property.

Loan-to-value: The loan's value divided by the property's appraised value.

Market study: Estimation of future demand for particular real estate projects, including possible rental fees and square feet sold or leased.

Market value: The sales price a property can command in a competitive market; the MV may or may not be the same as the appraisal value.

Minimum property requirements: Conditions property must meet before the Federal Housing Administration will underwrite a mortgage. The home must be reliably built, habitable, and up to housing standards in its location.

Mortgage: A loan given to buy a piece of property in which the property deed is held as collateral.

Normal wear and tear: Normal degradation of property with time and usage. It involves things such as small scratches on countertops or tramping down of carpet.

Observed condition: A way to appraise how much value a property has lost by assessing how much it has degraded, lost function, or grown obsolete relative to surrounding areas.

Obsolescence: Lessened value in property because it is outdated, whether because its components functions less well or it cannot compare with surrounding property.

Offer and acceptance: Needed for a successful real estate sale contract.

Operating expenses: The expenses incurred to keep the property maintained (utilities, maintenance, taxes).

Physical life: Predicted time period that buildings or other structures on real estate will last or remain livable.

Presale: Allows people to buy homes or other structures that are planned but not yet built.

Preservation district: Zoned to conserve wildernesses and beaches, as well as managed forests, grazing sites, and historic or picturesque spots.

Principle of conformity: States that properties are worth more if they resemble others nearby in their dimensions, appearance, functionality, and age.

Public auction: A meeting where the public gathers to buy property seized from a borrower, to pay off a defaulted mortgage.

Private mortgage insurance (PMI): A type of insurance required on mortgage loans with less than 20 percent equity. The insurance covers the lender's costs should the borrower default on the loan. It does not protect the borrower.

Range of value: The spectrum of prices a piece of real estate might be worth on the market.

Real estate owned (REO): Real property a lender or savings institution receives because of a foreclosure.

Recapture rate: To an appraiser, this means the rate at which someone recovers invested money.

Refinancing: Using one loan to pay off another loan.

Seller's market: Occurs when demand for real estate rises or supply drops, allowing sellers to charge more.

Short sale: Occurs when an owner sells property but the proceeds do not pay off his mortgage. The lender lets the remaining debt go, opting for less money and avoiding a foreclosure.

Spot zoning: Designating one parcel of land for different uses than other zoned property around it — an act courts might prohibit.

Square-foot method: Approximating the cost of improvements by counting the proposed square feet and multiplying by the price for one square foot of the type of construction planned.

Structural defects: Harm to the parts of a house bearing its weight. Structural defect make property less habitable, and they arise from earthquakes, sinkholes, and other forces shifting the ground.

Structural density: Comparison between how much floor space a building has and the lot's area. A typical industrial building has a structural density of 1 to 3, meaning its land area is three times its floor space.

Turnkey project: Has someone besides the owner in charge of building or improving a structure — for example, a project the developer finishes to the last detail. Also, a purchased property already stocked with furnishings or other objects is a turnkey property.

Walk-up: A tall apartment complex where people must use the stairs for lack of an elevator.

Write-off: In accounting, this means an asset lost because it cannot be collected.

Author

Biography

Maurcia DeLean Houck is a nationally known writer and editor with more than 1,500 bylines in 250 such well-known publications as *First for Women, Family Life, Writer's Digest, Your Health, AAA Going Places* and *Modern Woman*. She began her freelance career in 1991 while still serving as the executive editor of a mid-sized weekly newspaper in Philadelphia. She has also worked as a staff writer at several suburban newspapers in and around the Philadelphia area.

From 2001 to 2004, Houck expanded her interests in marketing and PR to include large scale fundraising as both a PR Assistant for the Phoenixville Area YMCA during their most recent $50 million Capital Campaign, and as a Development Assistant for West-Mont Christian Academy in Pottstown. She

also worked closely with Crandall & Associates, a national Fundraising Organization in 2004, to develop and implement a series of fundraising seminars for non-profit organizations in and around the tri-state area. Her work with the organization continues as an Associate Grant Writer.

In addition to her work as a freelance writer, publicist, and fundraising professional, Ms. Houck periodically reviews and edits current titles for Augsburg Fortress Publishing House, as well as a variety of private authors. Houck is a 1999-2000 and 2000-2001 Inductee in Who's Who in the East and a former member of the National Writer's Association (1994-1999).

An established nonfiction author, Houck has had the following books published:

But I Do not Know How To Start A Publicity Ministry in My Church (Warner Press 2001)

If These Walls Could Talk ... A Guide to Tracking the Genealogy of Your Historic Home (Picton Press 1999)

The Grandparent's Answer Guide (Chariot-Victor 2000 collaborator).

The Writer's Life (The Writer, Inc. 1998 collaborator)

Family Travel Guides (Carousel Press 1995)

Index